THE SOVEREIGN AND THE SUFFERING

Hurting Hearts in the Hands of a Loving God

David Jeremiah

with Dr. David Jeremiah

with Dr. David Jeremiah

© 2010 Turning Point for God
P.O. Box 3838
San Diego, CA 92163
All Rights Reserved

Editorial and Design Services:
Mark Gilroy Creative, LLC with ThinkPen Design, Inc.

www.markgilroy.com
www.thinkpendesign.com

Contributing Writers Robert J. Morgan and Weston Albert

Printed in the United States of America.

The Sovereign and The Suffering

Hurting Hearts in the Hands of a Loving God

David Jeremiah

TABLE OF CONTENTS

INTRODUCTION

An old African proverb claims, "Smooth seas do not make skillful sailors." We love smooth seas and sunny days; and if we had our way, there would be no storms, no clouds, no sorrows, and no losses. But Jesus said, "In the world you will have tribulation" (John 16:33), so we'd better learn to be good sailors.

The weather may change quickly. Without warning, we can face devastating circumstances, including the loss of our homes, of those dear to us, of money and possessions, of health, of employment, and of hope. Just read the Book of Job! Like a succession of tidal waves, misfortune slammed into Job's life, and he was left treading waters of unfathomable pain.

We're all potential Jobs. We're living in a world that can change rapidly—one terrorist act, one natural disaster, one economic collapse, one nuclear weapon, and our planet will never be the same. But our individual lives are just as fragile. The roof over our head may be gone tomorrow. The money in our pocket may vanish. Those dear to us now may be missing in the future. The Bible says we are living in perilous times, and Jesus warned, "In the world you will have tribulation."

But in that verse—John 16:33—Jesus didn't close His mouth and stop talking at the end of that phrase. There's not a period after the word "tribulation." In my Bible, there's a semicolon: "In the world you will have tribulation; but be of good cheer, I have overcome the world."

Praise God for that semicolon! All our losses are temporary; all our blessings are permanent. In the power of Jesus Christ, we are more than conquerors. Nothing can separate us from His love. All things work together for good. Those who wait upon Him will renew their strength, and we can do all things through Him who strengthens us. We can even "count it all joy."

Here's the full quote from John 16:33: "These things I have spoken to you, that in Me you may have peace. In the world you will have tribulation; but be of good cheer, I have overcome the world." Before the word "tribulation" is "peace," and after the word "tribulation" is "cheer." Jesus Himself is the opening and closing: "I have spoken" and "I have overcome." And we are "in Him"!

Dr. J. I. Packer wrote in his book *Knowing God*:

> We should not, therefore, be too taken aback when unexpected and upsetting and discouraging things happen to us now. What do they mean? Why, simply that God in His wisdom means to make something of us which we have not attained yet, and is dealing with us accordingly....
>
> It is often the case, as all the saints know, that fellowship with the Father and the Son is most vivid and sweet, and Christian joy the greatest, when the cross is heaviest.

Packer then suggests two ways of handling the trials of life when we cannot, for the moment, see God's purpose in them. "First, by taking them as from God, and asking ourselves what reactions to them, and in them, the Gospel of God requires of us; second, by seeking God's face specifically about them. If we do these two things, we shall never find ourselves wholly in the dark as to God's purpose in troubles."[1]

I've written this book to help us do those things in distressing times. Each chapter includes a personal story from people who encountered

---

1   J. I. Packer, *Knowing God* (Downers Grove, IL: Intervarsity, 1973), 86–87.

difficulty and despair, but found hope, comfort, and encouragement from their loving God during those times. There is suffering in life; that's inescapable. But God is sovereign, and that's undeniable. He is our refuge and strength, a very present help in trouble. Whatever you're going through, you are not alone. Tribulation is universal; but it's temporary for the believer; and it's surrounded by peace and cheer—and by Christ.

The apostle Peter, praising God for this, wrote, "Blessed be the God and Father of our Lord Jesus Christ, who according to His abundant mercy has begotten us again to a living hope through the resurrection of Jesus Christ from the dead. . . . In this you greatly rejoice, though now for a little while, if need be, you have been grieved by various trials, that the genuineness of your faith, being much more precious than gold that perishes, though it is tested by fire, may be found to praise, honor, and glory at the revelation of Jesus Christ, whom having not seen you love" (1 Peter 1:3-8).

If you're on stormy seas, you have a Captain for your faith and an anchor for your soul. If you're facing suffering, you have an Almighty Sovereign. If you have burdens, you also have a Bible. If your Bible warns of tribulation, it also promises peace and good cheer. Don't give up in rough waters. Learn to be a good sailor and to sing over the billows:

> *Jesus, Savior, pilot me*
> *Over life's tempestuous sea;*
> *Unknown waves before me roll,*
> *Hiding rock and treacherous shoal.*
> *Chart and compass come from Thee;*
> *Jesus, Savior, pilot me.*[2]

---

2   Edward Hopper, "Jesus, Savior, Pilot Me."

CHAPTER 1

Foreclosed and Forlorn— Rebuilding From the Loss of a Home

But He knows the way that I take; when He has tested me,
I shall come forth as gold. My foot has held fast to His steps;
I have kept His way and not turned aside.

JOB 23:10-11

THE SOVEREIGN

The righteous cry out, and the LORD hears,
and delivers them out of all their troubles.
The LORD is near to those who have a broken heart,
and saves such as have a contrite spirit.
Many are the afflictions of the righteous,
but the LORD delivers him out of them all.

PSALM 34:17-19

"Loss" is such a little word, just four letters most often seen on the sports pages of the newspaper. But few words treat us more cruelly. We meet it early in life as the loss of a toy or a pet often represents our first heartaches. The loss of a championship game can reduce athletes of all ages to unruly tears. The most seasoned executives tremble when seeing heavy loss on their financial statements. An election "loss" can end a politician's career.

In times of difficulty we talk about cutting our losses, being at a loss, and or facing total loss. In time of bereavement, people tell us they're sorry for our loss. If only we could erase that word *loss* from the dictionary of our lives!

Losing a home is a deeply traumatic loss; it takes a heavy toll on our mental and emotional well-being. Just ask Ethelda Lopez. According to newspaper accounts, Ethelda and her family began having financial struggles when her monthly retirement checks stopped. The Sacramento accounting firm managing her retirement and investment accounts disappeared overnight; the company's phone lines went dead. Things began unraveling quickly. Ethelda had worked for AT&T for thirty years; but now without her retirement check, she was unable to make the mortgage payments on the family's one-story ranch home.

She made hundreds of calls to mortgage companies, federal officials, political leaders, and bank managers. Too ashamed to tell her friends what was happening, she cried herself to sleep night after night. In the end, Ethelda stood on the lawn of the county courthouse in Merced, California, and watched her dream home being auctioned off. "When I heard my address, it was so disheartening," she said. "When I started to try to tell my story, it would just come out as crying. I was too embarrassed, too depressed to go out anymore. It's very trying. I would never wish this on anyone."[3]

Ethelda isn't alone. One in seven homes in her county has been foreclosed on since September of 2006, and the crisis is global. Untold thousands of homeowners around the world are hanging by a thread, trying to figure out how to pay mortgages on dwellings worth less now than what they owe. Roughly two million homes in America have been lost to foreclosure over the past two years, and another three million may be on the way.

Losing a home is a deeply traumatic loss; it takes a heavy toll on our mental and emotional well-being.

Of course, there are other ways to lose a home. Mudslides can literally send a house careening down a mountainside like a sled. Thousands of Haitians lost their homes in the 2010 earthquake, from the

3   This account comes from several articles by Danielle E. Gaines of McClatchy Newspapers, including "From Courthouse Steps, Woman Sees Dream Home Dissolve" on February 3, 2010, in *The Tribune of San Luis Obispo*, at http://www.sanluisobispo.com/business/national/story/1014087.html, accessed February 3, 2010.

Presidential Palace to the hovels in the alleys. Millions of people are pushed out of their homes every year by divorce, disability, old age, or changing fortunes.

Much of our comfort and security in life is found beneath our shingles.

Much of our comfort and security in life is found beneath our shingles. Whether we live in a tent or a mansion, an apartment or a townhouse, we need a place to call our own. That's where we retreat from the world, insulate ourselves from the cold (literally and metaphorically), eat, sleep, entertain ourselves, manage our lives, entertain our friends, enjoy our families, and get a good night's sleep.

That's an awful lot to lose.

JESUS LOVES YOU

If "loss" is your middle name right now—especially if that loss involves a home—I offer you all the sympathy and love in the world. Such loss can't be minimized, but we can support one another in difficult times. And I'm convinced that the Lord Jesus is still on the throne, He still cares for His people, and He still loves you.

Tell yourself this: "Jesus loves me, this I know, for the Bible tells me so."

That song, in fact, was written by two women who knew what it was to lose their home. It happened in the Financial Panic of 1837. Anna and Susan Warner were living with their father, Henry Warner, in an elegant home on St. Mark's Place in New York City. They enjoyed New York's high society; and their home was filled with expensive furniture, exquisite paintings, and accessories of every kind. Cooks, maids, coachmen, gardeners, and tutors waited at their disposal.

When the economy collapsed, Henry's high-flying world crashed. His investments soured, his wealth evaporated, and his debt mushroomed. The elegant home at St. Mark's was lost, along with most of their possessions and furnishings. Henry moved his family into a drafty old house on barren Constitution Island, upriver from New York City. He never recovered financially or emotionally. Even the few items he salvaged were seized and auctioned off, and the family was saddled with impossible debts that plagued them for decades.

His daughters, Anna and Susan, realized they had to contribute to the family's income, so they began writing. At first, the girls found no publisher interested in their work, but then George Putnam took a chance on one of Susan's novels, *The Wide, Wide World*, and their careers took off.

All told, the Warner sisters wrote 106 books and helped pioneer the field of modern Christian fiction. As dedicated followers of Christ, they built their stories around Gospel truth. In 1860, the sisters coauthored a book entitled *Say and Seal*, a Victorian-era romance about a high school teacher and a lovely local girl. Anna wrote a poem that was woven into the story, and the words said, "Jesus loves me, this I know. . . . " The book became a bestseller, and Christian composer William Bradbury soon composed music for the poem. The rest is history.[4]

I've related this story because it's an example that even the loss of a home isn't outside God's overruling providence. The Bible tells us that all things work together for good to those who love Him (Romans 8:28); and while that verse isn't a quick-fix for our problems, it is an unfailing promise for the people of God in their various trials and troubles.

4   This information comes from Robert J. Morgan's book, *Jesus Loves Me, This I Know*, published by J. Countryman (Nashville: Thomas Nelson, 2006), 49–60.

God's plans for us aren't thwarted by floods, fires, mudslides, or foreclosures. According to Ephesians 1:11-12 (NIV), He "works out everything in conformity with the purpose of His will, in order that we, who were the first to hope in Christ, might be for the praise of His glory."

Even our Lord Jesus Christ said, "Foxes have holes and birds of the air have nests, but the Son of Man has nowhere to lay His head" (Luke 9:58). He not only left His heavenly home but He was often bereft of an earthly one, all in order to provide a home for our faith now, and an eternal mansion for us in glory.

A HOME IMPERISHABLE

Many of us are fortunate to have thus far avoided the loss of hearth and home. But the brutal truth is this: Sooner or later, we're all going to be moved out of our houses. It might be on a stretcher. Though it sounds depressing to say, someone else will be living in our homes one day. Someone else will walk through our rooms, eat at our tables, gaze at our paintings, and sleep in our beds. We're not yet in permanent dwellings. This world is not our home, and not even the wealthiest man in the world has a lasting deed to his mansion. Jesus said about the rich man who continually expanded his property and goods, "Fool! This night your soul will be required of you; then whose will those things be which you have provided?" (Luke 12:20).

> This world is not our home. Not even the wealthiest man in the world has a lasting deed to his mansion.

In his book *Walden,* Henry David Thoreau took a dim view of estate sales. He said that the people in his village spent years accumulating things needing to be dusted. When one of these people died, all their things were carted to the town square to be auctioned off to other people who would have to spend their lives dusting them.

No, I'm not belittling the loss of our possessions. My wife and I have many possessions we value, and some of them provide price-less memories of precious times. But we can become too attached to the things of the world, whereas an old hymn rightly tells us instead to "build our hopes on things eternal" and "hold to God's unchanging hand."

Jesus said, "In My Father's house are many mansions; if it were not so, I would have told you. I go to prepare a place for you" (John 14:2). Just think! The Carpenter of Nazareth is busy right now building mansions for His people.

We read in Genesis about the patriarch Abraham, who left the city of Ur of the Chaldeans because God was relocating him to another place. Abraham probably occupied a fabulous home in Ur. Extensive excavations have been mounted in that ancient site, and many of the artifacts are now in the British Museum in London. If Abraham was a well-regarded resident of his city, he likely enjoyed a comfortable two-story brick house with a lobby, courtyard, kitchen and bathroom, bedrooms, and reception room.[5]

In the providence and will of God, Abraham and Sarah lost their beautiful home. The Bible says, "By faith (Abraham) dwelt in the land of promise as in a foreign country, dwelling in tents . . . for he waited for the city which has foundations, whose builder and maker is God" (Hebrews 11:9-10).

---

5   Brian Edwards and Clive Anderson, *Through the British Museum – with the Bible* (Leominster, England: Day One Publications, 2004), 27.

We're looking for a city of gold and mansions in glory. The loss
of a home is traumatic, but when our families come through it, still
having their health and love, it makes the loss bearable. It equips us
to minister to others with fresh insights. And it forces us to seek those
things that are above, where Christ is, sitting at the right hand of God.

He is our Sovereign, even in times of suffering. There's no easy
answer to being foreclosed and forlorn; few things are more
protracted or painful. But in Jesus Christ we have a home that
outshines the sun, an inheritance that can never perish, spoil, or
fade, and treasures that can never rust or be stolen. The deed of our
heavenly home is signed and sealed with the blood of Christ; the
contract is ratified by the Resurrection. And no one will ever fore-
close on that.

THE SUFFERING

Personal Story—David Rhoads

*M*any people dream of having the perfect home, transitioning from being a tenant to an owner. In many ways, owning a house has become part of the American dream. Our homes express a great deal about us; some homeowners keep their belongings immaculately organized, others create a personalized look with artwork, while others use furnishings to establish a cozy space. Our homes are a place of memories: the conversations over coffee, children playing catch in the front yard, family dinners at the table. But what if your house was suddenly taken away from you—the place once filled by the warmth of people, now empty and cold? What would you do? How would losing your home reverberate through your life?

Sitting in a small bedroom and looking through a window at the house that was once his home, David Rhoads pondered the same questions.

In 2006, David and his wife left behind their friends, family, and an 800-square-foot condominium in San Diego to move to Savannah, Georgia. Moving provided them the opportunity to buy a large, beautiful home with the hopes of starting a family. It seemed perfect when they bought it. David was proud—delighted that he now owned a spacious home he could call his own. But what began as a wonderful opportunity would soon become an encumbrance.

After living in Georgia for two years, David made a difficult choice to leave his position at their church. He believed resigning was the moral and God-honoring decision, disagreeing with activities going on within the congregation. Yet, resigning his position also left him without the paycheck that was the primary income for his family—leaving David to search for work in a struggling economy. When he finally found a job, the pay was much less than he had been making at his previous position. As David struggled to pay the bills, especially the mortgage, he began to question his value and ability to support his family. Money had always been a source of tension in David's marriage, but the extra financial shortfall sent the couple into a tailspin. Suddenly, the move to Georgia seemed all wrong.

David and his wife were determined to keep their home from falling into foreclosure. Attempting to sell the home through both traditional and a short-sale, they pursued every option. While David and his wife were in the midst of attempting to dig out of the financial hole they were in, exhausting all their options to sell the home, the bank foreclosed on them. After six months of emotional turmoil, it was finally over. The mortgage-induced burden David had been living under for the past several months finally lifted, and he was relieved—especially when the bank sold the property for the amount that was owed. Unfortunately though, the financial trials had taken their toll on David's marriage, and he and his wife later divorced.

Without a place to stay, David's neighbor offered him a spare bedroom. It was a blessing, but David now lived across the street from his former home, facing the house that he had struggled to keep. It was a constant reminder of the life he had and everything he had lost. He watched from the borrowed room as people toured the property, frustrated at the number of prospective buyers who visited when he had tried so hard to sell and received so little interest. David stayed in Savannah a little while longer, and then swallowed his pride and called his parents. In this difficult phone call home he explained that he had little of anything and was without a job, and asked if he could move back in with them in San Diego. It was a huge blow to David's ego after being on his own for twenty years, but returning to the support system of his youth was a good decision.

While thankful for his parents' generosity and support, over time David wanted to get out on his own again—fighting discouragement that came with the opinions and questions he received from people who wondered why he was living in his parents' house, unable to support himself. He knew it wouldn't be easy with a foreclosure on his record and years ahead of him to restore his credit, but David wanted desperately to get back on his feet, earn his independence again, and build up his financial security. After months of searching diligently for work, he finally found a job. David is now back to work and on the path to restoring his life.

Learning to be content with what you have, rather than needing the best or most expensive possessions, is perhaps the greatest lesson David has learned. Getting caught up in the American dream, feeding his ego with possessions he could barely afford, took him from having everything he thought he wanted back to the things he really needed. Having had and lost, he doesn't define himself anymore by the belongings he owns. God has taught him to be content in Him and trust that He will supply his needs. He has experienced God's devotion even in the midst of disaster in his life.

Difficult circumstances have brought David closer to God than he has been in years. He has been studying God's Word and pursuing a deeper relationship with Him. Much of David's career was spent preaching and teaching God and His Word to other people, but now he is able to encounter God personally, the way he had instructed

others to do for so long. David feels God's presence during the after-
math of foreclosure and divorce—so much so that he is filled with
joy—a testament to God's working in his life. This change in perspective and attitude would not be possible without God working in his
life. David's friends and family are amazed at God's material provision for David, but they marvel at the spiritual and emotional growth
they see. Now, rather than dwelling on the past in self-pity and
depression, David looks to the future with a genuine smile because he
recognizes God's faithfulness, even in his brokenness.

David recalls that there are still moments of indecision, "Of course,
I sometimes close the doors at night and roll up in a ball—you have
those times by yourself, but there are more joyous times than those."

David is finally beginning to see himself emerge from the valley of
his suffering. He has reconnected with friends that have long been
out of contact, including former students he taught as teenagers. He
has been offered the opportunity to live in a home that is for sale
during this slow housing market by friends who want their property
to look occupied. God is providing for him in unexpected ways.

The biggest lesson through this season of hardship has been
humility. If someone had said a year previous that David would
have a foreclosed house, only a small amount of possessions, and be
divorced and living with his parents, no one would have believed
it, especially David. But our lives can change drastically in a short
time. Sometimes it only takes one decision—or one incident we can't
control—to alter the course of everything we have planned out in
detail. David now approaches everything, especially important decisions, with meekness, having been humbled by his circumstances.
David never saw this hard time coming, but he knows great things

are coming in his future. And he is filled with the comfort that he received from God's help, even in his hurting.

We sometimes think that if we don't have the most luxurious vehicle, extravagant house, or trendsetting clothes, we will look foolish to the people around us. We let our possessions define us, and they become a status symbol among our peers. But how much more foolish will we look when all those things are stripped away in a moment, and we are left with nothing? The loss of a home can be incredibly discomforting and upsetting, but we do not have to hide our embarrassment from God. He is our shelter in the time of storm—He has promised to take care of us, and He is faithful to do so in ways we cannot imagine or think.

CHAPTER 2

Taken Too Soon—Discovering Mercy After the Loss of a Child

So the ransomed of the LORD shall return, and come to Zion with singing, with everlasting joy on their heads. They shall obtain joy and gladness; sorrow and sighing shall flee away.

ISAIAH 51:11

THE SOVEREIGN

Therefore you now have sorrow;
but I will see you again and
your heart will rejoice, and your joy
no one will take from you.

JOHN 16:22

On October 18, 1982, Dr. Earl McQuay taught his regular seminary class of ministry students at Columbia International University in South Carolina, explaining to them the stages of grief. He particularly wanted to equip his students to deal with parents in the loss of a child, and he read aloud the heart-tugging testimony of a father whose son, a strapping young man, had died following heart surgery.

After class, Dr. McQuay proceeded to the college dining room and was just about to take his first bite of lunch when a secretary appeared by his side. "Dr. McQuay," she said, "you have an emergency phone call from North Carolina." McQuay's heart skipped a beat; his own son, Tim, a newly-married medical student, was in North Carolina. The news was tragic. While trying to insert a tape into his car's sound system, Tim had lost control of the vehicle. He was not expected to survive.

Dr. and Mrs. McQuay rushed to North Carolina, and that night in the hospital chapel they knelt in great pain and with many tears. Lifting their hands to God, they prayed, "Lord, when Tim was a baby we held him up to You and gave him to You. And we have main-tained that commitment through the twenty-three years of his life.

Again now we lift him to You. You are our Sovereign Lord, and Your plan is perfect. . . ."

Tim passed away, and nothing could have prepared the McQuays for the ensuing grief and anguish. Dr. McQuay later wrote, "The theological side of me declares, 'Tim is alive in heaven and all is well. Rejoice!' But there is a humanly frail side of me that cries, 'My dear son is gone. And I miss him so!' I know that separation is only temporary. Yet I hurt deeply. My strength fails. Dark clouds hide the sun. I feel alone. My heart cries for my son."

"THE CHILD IS NOT DEAD"

Perhaps no one should write on this subject who hasn't gone through such an experience; yet all of us are touched by the death of a child and none of us want to experience the grief of losing a youngster. From the moment our children are born, we worry about "something happening to them." Some couples lose a child even before birth, through miscarriage, stillbirth, or, in some cases, abortion. Others have only a few minutes or hours before their baby is taken home by God. Some children succumb to fatal diseases or encounter tragic accidents early in life. Teens die in car wrecks. Young men and women lay down their lives in military service and are buried in flag-draped coffins. No one is exempt. Questions linger, and our Whys? are not always answered.

Yet we know from Scripture that God loves children and He loves babies. He loves the preborn and He loves the newborn. He loves the infant and He loves the toddler. The very words *child* and *children* occur ninety-four times in the Gospels alone, telling us they are as important as any other element in the story of Jesus. "Let the little children come to Me," our Lord said in Matthew 19:14, "and do not forbid them; for of such is the kingdom of heaven."

Jesus gave His true perspective concerning the death of children in a very special verse of Scripture, Mark 5:39. Standing over the corpse of a recently-deceased twelve-year-old, He declared, "The child is not dead, but sleeping." The wailing mourners laughed Him to scorn, but Jesus went into the death room, knelt by the body, and said to her in Aramaic, "Talitha, cumi" ("Little girl, get up!" NIV). Her life returned, and she rose and was restored to her overjoyed parents.

The Bible offers unique comfort to grieving parents, and I believe Scripture teaches that those who die in childhood are saved and taken to heaven. In 2 Samuel 12, King David was inconsolable while his young child was deathly ill. He fasted and prayed, prostrating himself day and night on the ground, pleading with God. But within seven days, the infant died. Hearing the news whispered about, David rose, bathed, dressed, and went to the Lord's house to worship. When asked about it, he replied, "I shall go to him, but he shall not return to me" (2 Samuel 12:23).

The Bible offers unique comfort to grieving parents.

Since David obviously expected to "dwell in the house of the Lord forever" (Psalm 23:6), he comforted himself by knowing his son was with the Lord awaiting the day of happy reunion.

I also think Isaiah 57:1 is a comforting verse for those mourning the loss of one who seems to have died too young. It's put this way in *The Living Bible:* "Good people pass away; the godly often die before their time. But no one seems to care or wonder why. No one seems to understand that God is protecting them from the evil to come." Perhaps God takes some people home to heaven in their youth to spare them from some looming evil which He alone, in His omniscient sovereignty, can foresee.

I also think there's great comfort in 2 Kings 4:26. This is the story of the Shunammite woman whose son suffered a brain seizure and died. After having her boy carried to the guest room, the woman left to see the prophet Elisha. The man of God was surprised to see the Shunammite woman approaching in the distance, and he sent word, "Is it well with you? Is it well with your husband? Is it well with the child?"

And she answered, "It is well."

In one sense, it was most certainly *not* well, for her son was dead; yet it *was* well with the child. It was well because the boy was safe in the arms of God. Elisha later raised the child to life; but even in her moment of grief, this mother understood, "It is well." (You might also be interested to learn this is the sentence in the Bible that comforted Horatio Spafford when his four daughters perished in the sinking of the *S.S. Ville du Havre,* and which led to his writing the great hymn, "It is Well with My Soul.")

CHILDREN WHO DIE GO TO HEAVEN

John MacArthur, in his book on this subject, wrote, "Little children . . . have no basis on which to believe or not believe. They are incapable of discerning right from wrong, sin from righteousness, and evil from goodness. Scripture is very clear on this truth. Little children have no record of unbelief or evil works, and therefore, there is no basis for their deserving an eternity apart from God. As innocents, they are graciously and sovereignly saved by God as part of the atoning work of Jesus Christ."[6]

The great theologian of Geneva, John Calvin, wrote: "Those little children have not yet any understanding to desire His blessing, but when they are presented to Him, He gently and kindly receives them, and dedicates them to the Father by a solemn act of blessing. It would be too cruel (to exclude that age from the grace of redemption)."

The great British preacher Charles Spurgeon put it this way in his sermon entitled "The Way of Salvation."

> Are (infants) saved, and if so, how? I answer, saved they are beyond a doubt; all children dying in infancy are caught away to dwell in the third heaven of bliss forever. . . . We believe that they are all saved—every one of them without exception—but not apart from the one great sacrifice of the Lord Jesus Christ.[7]

WHAT HELPS US

Some time after Tim's death, Dr. Earl McQuay wrote a small book entitled *Beyond Eagles: A Father's Grief and Hope,* in which he listed five realities that provided immense comfort to his heart, and to his wife's.

First was Scripture. The infallible Word of God served as firm ground on which to withstand the hurricane of tragedy that swept over their souls. They found verses, claimed promises, studied the truths about heaven, and drew near to the Lord day by day within the covers of His Book.

6   John MacArthur, *Safe in the Arms of God* (Nashville, Thomas Nelson, 2003), p. 81.

7   Charles Spurgeon, in his sermon "The Way of Salvation," at http://www.spurgeon.org/sermons/0209.htm, accessed December 15, 2005.

Second was prayer. They could cry out before the throne of God, knowing He sympathized with their weaknesses, and they felt the support of many others who were praying for them. In prayer we crawl into God's arms, rest in His presence, pour out our hearts to Him, and trust Him to turn our heartaches into Hallelujahs.

Third, friends. "At the time of our greatest need," wrote McQuay, "the members of the body of Christ came to our relief. Their many cards, letters, flowers, food, memorial gifts, calls and prayers encouraged us and aided the healing process."

Fourth, memories. Dr. McQuay and his wife relished the twenty-three years they had enjoyed with Tim. Nothing could take away those smiles, laughs, and good times.

Finally, hope. For the Christian, death is not a period but a comma in the story, only a pause; and all our separations are temporary. Christians only part to meet again.[8]

> Our time on earth is but a wink and a flash. But our God is from everlasting to everlasting, and He has prepared a place for us.

My words can never reduce a parent's pain, but I believe with all my heart that God's Words can impart eternal comfort. He who said, "Let the little children come to Me," is preparing an everlasting city where friendships will never end, relationships will never sour, separations will never divide, and death will never intrude. Our time on earth is but a wink and a flash, and then we're gone. But our God is from everlasting to everlasting, and He has prepared a place for us.

Let's comfort one another with His Words.

---

8   [8] The quotes and insights from Dr. Earl McQuay come from his book, *Beyond Eagles: A Father's Grief and Hope* (Columbus, GA: Grill Publications, 1987), passim.

THE SUFFERING

Personal Story—Denny Stover

*I*t is the phone call that every parent dreads. On April 1, 2009, Denny Stover received that life-changing call from a friend, advising him to get in touch with his sixteen-year-old son, Christian—he heard there had been an accident. Denny had spoken to Christian just a few hours before when his son called to ask if he could ride his ATV (a four-wheeled all-terrain vehicle) with a friend. The worried father began dialing frantically, and eventually contacted the fire captain in the area where Christian was riding. The captain told Denny devastating news—Christian was in an accident and hadn't made it. He hit his head on a rock after being thrown from his ATV. The attempts by rescuers to revive Christian were unsuccessful. The news was crippling. This precious son who had brought so much joy and happiness to his parents and family was gone. He was taken too soon.

When Christian was a toddler, Denny couldn't wait for the day he could pull out his baseball glove and teach Christian the game he had grown up playing. Sometimes our dreams are attained through our children, so Denny was eager to get a ball and bat into his son's hands, and turn him into the ball player that he never was. As Christian grew older, he played baseball, but he soon found his own passion—racing.

After watching a friend racing go-karts, Christian asked his dad if he could try it. Denny said he could, but mostly ignored Christian's request, thinking he was just being a kid asking for a new toy, and his desire would soon go away. But it didn't—his requests only grew more persistent. So Denny took him to a driving school to see if he would really like go-kart racing and if it was something he wanted to realistically pursue. Christian got behind the wheel and hit the asphalt track. He loved it and had a strong desire to race competitively, so his parents bought him a go-kart. Denny did not know anything about go-karts or racing—it was far from the simplicity of a well-worn mitt and ball he knew so well, so without a mechanical bone in his body, he set off on a journey with his son to follow his passion.

After hundreds of practice laps, Christian raced in his first go-kart competition when he was eight years old. His eyes lit up when he raced, and Denny knew it was time to put away the baseball bat and pick up a wrench. Learning the mechanics of the kart, Denny began working on the vehicles for his son. Christian won several races locally in the San Diego area and then he and his dad began traveling to regional competitions. It could be said that Christian was a natural, which was evidenced as he continued to amass wins and won a national title when he was ten. At eleven years old, he was competing—and winning—against drivers five years his senior. Everywhere there was a major go-kart race in the United States and Canada, Christian was there. Eventually, he even secured the sponsorship of an Italian company that wanted Christian to drive their karts in the States. Christian was introduced to a sprint car—a four-wheeled car with a 900-horsepower engine that drives on dirt—which he raced competitively until his death.

It comes as no surprise that Denny and his wife, Kim, were heartbroken at the loss of their son. Their faith was tested like never before. It is easy to have faith when life is going as expected and blessings are abundant, but it is an entirely different challenge to stay confident in the Lord when encountering something as overwhelming as the death of a child. Denny and Kim immediately got involved in Christian counseling to help deal with the tragedy—the hardest thing their family had ever faced. Difficult days followed, but the love and support of their close family and the Lord helped them through each day.

At Christian's funeral the family knew a lot of people were praying for them—they felt an incredible level of comfort even as they mourned their precious son. It wasn't really until after Christian's death that they came to realize how much of an impact their son had on those around him as hundreds of teenagers and adults came to Christian's funeral remembering the mark he had left on their lives. Denny was amazed when a number of hall-of-fame sprint car drivers from around the country attended the funeral to pay their respects to Christian. To this day the family continues to see Christian's reverberating influence in unexpected ways. Perhaps one of the most unexpected came during a recent baptism at Shadow Mountain Community Church. A woman stood before the congregation, dedicating her life to the Lord because she had heard the Gospel message while attending Christian's funeral with her son (who was a friend of Christian's). Denny takes those stories as reassurance from God that His hand was upon every moment of Christian's life. Knowing that Christian's legacy lives on gives the Stover family comfort. They are proud of the positive impact Christian made on everyone he came into contact with—representing himself, his family, and most importantly, the Lord in the way he lived his life.

As a father, Denny will always remember Christian's outgoing, bubbly personality and his love of life. The entire family misses his infectious smile and his humor that brought laughter into so many situations. Christian had an amazing ability to see the good in individuals. It has been hard to cope with losing such a bright light in their lives. At times the question has been asked of God—why did this need to happen? Denny and his wife recognize that there is a bigger plan—God's plan. Even though they don't understand the reasons why, Denny and Kim believe that everything will work out to glorify God, even Christian's death.

Through this difficult journey, Denny has learned that life is very precious. He now takes the time to appreciate what he has and who he is with at all times. He takes comfort that God is a Father and also experienced the loss of His Son. Just as God used Jesus to accomplish His perfect plan, Denny believes that Christian's death also fits into God's complex and sovereign plan, and will be used to reflect the majesty and splendor of the Lord. Denny may not fully understand why or how, but he has faith that God will use this tragedy to reach out to others, just as Christian reached out to people during his life. Denny and Kim are blessed with friends, family, and a community of believers surrounding them, constantly praying for them, as they also continue to ask the Lord for direction and guidance. Denny has been encouraged by the scriptural accounts of Jesus' reaction to His own death. Jesus wasn't looking forward to the crucifixion, but He submitted His will to the Father. Denny feels the same way. This isn't the way he would have written out Christian's or his family's life, but he acknowledges that this is God's plan. He has determined to get through this valley of sorrow to the best of his ability and to bring glory and honor to our Sovereign God whose love and plan is beyond our comprehension.

CHAPTER 3

Home Alone—Healing
After the Loss of a Spouse

Cast your burden on the LORD, and He shall sustain you;
He shall never permit the righteous to be moved.

PSALM 55:22

THE SOVEREIGN

Blessed be the God and Father of our LORD Jesus Christ,
the Father of mercies and God of all comfort, who comforts us
in all our tribulation, that we may be able to comfort those
who are in any trouble, with the comfort with which
we ourselves are comforted by God.

2 CORINTHIANS 1:3-4

Who do you suppose deserves the title of the most quoted preacher of the twentieth century? That description belongs to the North Carolina evangelist Vance Havner, the Southern revivalist who preached around the world, calling sinners to repentance and the church to revival. I quote from him often. Havner's dry wit and one-liners are legendary. He had a unique way of turning a phrase so that it tickled your ribs and pierced your heart, both at once. But his most popular and powerful book wasn't a volume of sermons or a collection of devotions. It was an account of his own personal anguish at losing his wife to a dreaded and fatal disease. Out of the crucible of suffering, he wrote *Though I Walk Through the Valley,* a book that contains no pat answers or time-worn clichés.

"No matter how one may condition himself for the passing of a dear one," Havner wrote, "no matter how many weeks or months you have to get ready for the actual moment, there comes the inevitable shock and the grim final blow when you realize that the one most precious is no longer here. I find myself saying under my breath again and again though ever so softly, 'Sara is gone.'

"Gone with her are a thousand other precious things that made the past years so delightful. Gone the anticipation of returning home to be greeted at the airport or the apartment door. Gone the thrill of hearing that voice at the other end of the telephone. . . . Gone those airmail letters in the motel box, one every day. Gone the clasp of that dear hand as we strolled about all over the country. Gone that lovely face in the congregation, smiling at my jokes she had heard countless times before."[9]

Gone.

Just like the word "loss," it's a four-letter word, cruel in its effect but unavoidable for pilgrims trudging through a world not their own. When a spouse dies, our world changes. Our daily routine changes. Our sleeping habits change. Our appetite and enjoyment of life are affected, and intense pain and loneliness come and go with no predictable patterns. There's no feeling as lonely as listening for a voice that no longer speaks or looking for the touch of a vanished hand.

> When a spouse dies, our world changes.

FROM COPING TO HOPING

My wife and I are still serving the Lord side-by-side; and I'm eternally thankful for that. Like most people, we've had health scares along the way, but God has preserved our lives. Yet we both know that, given enough time, one of us will likely be left alone someday, at least for a while until we're reunited in the Lord's presence. Like most people, we try to prepare for that day emotionally, spiritually, legally,

9 Vance Havner, *Though I Walk Through the Valley* (Old Tappen, NJ: Fleming H. Revell Co., 1974), 71.

and financially. The Bible tells us to "give thought to our steps." But losing a spouse is a trauma for which one can never prepare. As Havner said, "Only those who have traveled this road really know what the journey is like."[10]

That's true. But while I'm thankful to be excluded from this particular fellowship of suffering, I have, of course, lost those dear to me. And I've spent a lifetime ministering to so many whose loved ones have died. My church in California contains a vast number of widows and widowers of all ages, and my friendship with them gives me insights into their pain.

I've also carefully studied what the Bible says about this subject. God's great concern for us is seen in His constant commands to care for widows and widowers in their distress. It's remarkable how much ink is devoted to this in the Bible. Take a moment with me to trace this theme through the Scripture.

Think of how Abraham's grief is described when Sarah passed away. Genesis 23 says that he mourned for her and wept for her; and in anguish he purchased a small burial cave at the end of a field, and there he laid his beloved wife to rest near the town of Hebron.

Notice how often widows are mentioned in the Law of Moses, especially as it is related in Deuteronomy. The Old Testament laws contained multiple provisions and protections for those whose spouses had died. Israel's justice system was particularly keen to the rights and needs of widows.

Then we come to one entire book in the Bible devoted to the plight of two different women whose husbands had died—Naomi and Ruth. God's remarkable care and guidance over their lives set the stage for the subsequent redemptive history of Israel.

10   Ibid., 9.

One of the most unusual and instructive stories of the Old Testament concerns Elijah and the widow of Zarephath. During a time of famine, this widow's pantry was nearly empty, yet she shared what she had with Elijah. As a result, her bin of flour "was not used up, nor did the jar of oil run dry" (1 Kings 17:8-15). The stories of Elijah, Elisha, and the widows they met provide lessons about how God cares for those who have lost a loved one, and how He wants to use them as a blessing to others.

> Losing a spouse is a trauma for which one can never prepare.

The patriarch Job was devoted to helping those who had lost loved ones. He had a special ministry in this area. He said in Job 29:11-13, "Everyone who saw me or heard of me had good things to say about what I had done. When the poor cried out, I helped them; I gave help to orphans who had nowhere to turn . . . and I helped widows find security" (GNT).

The Book of Psalms is a rich source of comfort to us as we read, "A defender of widows is God in His holy habitation" (Psalm 68:5); and "The Lord . . . relieves the fatherless and widow" (Psalm 146:9).

Isaiah 54:5, which is sometimes called the "widow's verse," has bestowed infinite comfort to generations of grieving women: "For your Maker is your husband, the Lord of hosts is His name."

And think of our Lord's many encounters with widows. During the first days of His life, He was blessed by the prophetess Anna, a widow of eighty-four years; and during the last moments of His life, He made sure that His own widowed mother was provided for by the apostle John (John 19:16-27). In between these two widows were many others, including the famous widow who, in her poverty, placed her mite in the temple treasure and was commended by our Lord for her faithful generosity.

James tells us in his book that true religion is caring for those who have lost parents and spouses (James 1:27). And the Bible closes with two chapters describing the joy of resurrection, eternal life, and a city where there will be no more death, nor tears, nor sorrow, for the former things have passed away.

In times of great loss, we're also comforted with what the Bible says in its general teachings about death, resurrection, and eternal life.

WHAT TO DO

According to Christian counselors and grief therapists, it's important to mourn our loss and to give ourselves time to grieve. In her remarkable book, *To Live Again,* Catherine Marshall recalled her own struggles with forthright honesty. Her husband, Peter, Chaplain of the United States Senate, died suddenly of a heart attack. In the days immediately afterward, she said, "a Power outside myself lifted my spirit up and carried me steadily and surely through the necessary mechanics always connected with death."[11] But the weeks that followed were full of sobs, anger, irritation, rebellion, self-pity, despair, and every other emotion known to the human heart.

As time went by, the pain became slightly less intense; but one never knew when a tiny thing—anything—could bring it flooding back. The sight of his handwriting on a card shoved in the back of a drawer, someone on the street wearing a similar coat or hat, a familiar song, a certain smell, a pew at church now less crowded.

But Catherine learned that she could "live again," for the Lord, having not taken her yet, surely had work for her still to do. She

---

11   Catherine Marshall, *To Live Again* (New York: McGraw-Hill Book Company, Inc., 1957), 7.

discovered that a grieving heart needs work for the hands to do, and she got busy and stayed busy.

Oh, how important to call on God's omnipotent hand to pull us out of prolonged self-pitying depression!

We still have work to do.

We still have passages in the Bible to study.

We still have those who need us and depend on us.

We still have prayers to pray, and our prayer ministry can make the difference for those still remaining here below.

We can still trust God to meet our financial needs, to provide for us as we grow older, to walk beside us through the valley of the shadow, to be with us in sickness and in health.

We still need to be tough-minded optimists, knowing that Romans 8:28 didn't expire the moment our loved one died. God still does work all things together for our good.

And we still have heaven to anticipate and a day of reunion to think about. Each person finds solace in a different manner, but those who know God have the assurance that our lives are ordered by God day by day. The departing of our loved one is not a mistake on God's part or an accident of fate. God has the right to call us home whenever He chooses. He is Sovereign, and our times are in His hands.

> We still have heaven to anticipate and a day of reunion to think about.

So very often, John 14:28 has encouraged the one left behind. In that passage, spoken on the eve of His death, Jesus told His disciples: "If you loved Me, you would rejoice because I said, 'I am going to the Father.'"

Think of it as Jesus would. If we really loved our loved ones, we'd rejoice in their departure from the woes of this world. We'd rejoice in their walking the streets of glory. We'd rejoice in their seeing Jesus. We'd rejoice in their beating us to heaven. We'd rejoice in their wonder at experiencing the sights, sounds, colors, flowers, music, fellowship, and shimmering beauties of New Jerusalem.

I know it's hard for us to think in those terms; but it wasn't hard for Jesus. And as we walk with Him, He will take us in His good timing to Reunion City. We find infinite layers of never-ending comfort in that.

As Vance Havner put it in a prayer in the final paragraph of *Though I Walk Through the Valley:* "I have but one request, My Father. When I reach that distant shore, I can wait to see the pearly gates, the golden streets, and the many mansions. But grant, dear God, that after I have first seen Him, who having not seen I love, my dearest may be next to meet me, just like she used to do."

THE SUFFERING

Personal Story—Janet Waller

*I*magine waking up in the morning like any other day. You begin your normal morning routine—taking a shower, brushing your teeth, and having a cup of tea. On the way out the door for work, you bend down to kiss your spouse who is still sleeping and suddenly realize that something is wrong—the skin under your fingertips is cold. Shaking him brings no response and suddenly the tragic reality is understood: your spouse has passed away in the middle of the night. Your world suddenly shatters.

This was the experience of Janet Waller, whose husband, Donnie, never woke up from his sleep on New Year's Day 2006. Donnie's passing at only fifty-two was completely unexpected. The night before, Janet and Donnie had gone out to dinner with her children and enjoyed a wonderful time together, but the next morning Donnie did not wake up. Unbeknownst to anyone, Donnie had a brain tumor the size of a softball at the base of his neck, but had never showed any symptoms. He was here one second and gone the next. It was a traumatic loss for Janet. She hadn't even been able to say goodbye to him and was heartbroken at the loss of the man she loved so dearly.

Janet describes Donnie as a polite southern gentleman—she fondly remembers that he used to always open doors for her. He was a very loving and kind husband. He and Janet had been married (a remarriage for both of them) for about two and a half years before he passed away. Donnie loved the Lord and his family. He had a wonderful sense of humor, which was a real joy and balance for Janet, who was the more serious of the two. Donnie had a great appreciation for the countryside—a passion he developed being raised in Virginia. Janet shared his love of the outdoors—especially trees. They lived in a rural area of San Diego County, where they loved to walk and experience nature together. The couple enjoyed normal family activities: traveled on vacations, attended church, and just enjoyed spending time together each day.

Janet always thought of herself as a strong person, but knew that she would not be able to get through the death of her husband by herself. She had been thrust on a wild ride and now held on tight, experiencing a far deeper turmoil than she had ever known before. Her grief and crying continued past the point that tears ran dry. Questioning God as to her purpose on earth, she internalized her heartache in the form of depression. Feeling lost, Janet wondered what God had in store for her. Why had something so horrific happened? How could the Lord possibly use something so heart-wrenching for His purpose? Janet soon learned firsthand that God can use even the most tragic things in life for His good and help those who love Him. He would stir a spiritual growth in her that was formerly unimaginable.

Janet had been a Christian since she was young, but the death of her husband left her in shambles. It was impossible to open the Bible and read God's Word because of her relentless grief. But verses came to her memory, and she clung to them as her lifeline and promise from the Lord: "For I know the plans I have for you . . . plans to give you a future and a hope" (Jeremiah 29:11 RSV); and "God will never leave you nor forsake you" (Hebrews 13:5). In dire need of help, Janet remembered some realtors who had prayed for her and Donnie when they were looking for a house two years previously, so she picked up the phone and called them. This simple act lead Janet to a small group Bible study where she learned about Shadow Mountain Community Church—the church she now calls home. And through the church, Janet was able to join grief counseling. She began to fill her life with reminders of the Lord and began listening to worship music in the car. Even though she struggled with the pain of losing her husband, Janet refused to be bitter toward God. Knowing that God had some-thing to teach her, she was determined to learn it. She told herself to muster everything she could, even if it was only faith the size of a mustard seed. Rallying all the belief in her spirit, she found that with just that small kernel of trust, the Lord came through for her.

She was committed to keeping a perspective that honored the Lord. Asking God why He had taken Donnie seemed disrespectful because He is the Creator and God of the universe, and to question God's decisions felt like doubting His authority. Overcoming her fear of the Bible, Janet pulled back its cover and started reading. Now she reads it every day, getting up every morning at 3:30 to dive into its pages. She can't get enough of it. The stories have come alive for her, speaking to her soul, and becoming a part of her story. Another step to her perseverance and finding comfort within the Lord has been to journal, which has helped her develop a deeper, more personal rela-tionship with God. As she wrote her thoughts down and recounted her days on paper, a veil was lifted and God was visible and active, working in her life. Even though there is so much in life that is out of control, Janet came to understand the only thing she could control was her own attitude.

God has been a constant help through her sorrow. Janet amazingly doesn't cry over her loss anymore. Although still saddened by the death of her husband, she has a newfound joy in the Lord and revels in her relationship with Him. God has rewritten so much of Janet's life that in a strange and surprising way, she is almost thankful for the path that the Lord has set before her. It was a difficult and painful road to tread, but God worked in such a mighty way that Janet has been transformed by the love and comfort of her Heavenly Father.

Her greatest encouragement in this tragedy has been her walk with God. She knows that God is with her and loves her—He knows the numbers of hairs on her head. The promises found in the Bible provide her with confidence and hope as she continues on her walk of faith. The Lord has an awesome plan for Janet, and she awaits His leading. She has experienced the Lord's willing care for those who trust in Him, and His blessings which pour out even to those in distress.

Janet has come to see her budding relationship with the Lord like the trees she climbed and played in as a girl. Before her husband's death, the roots of her faith were slender and shallow. But now she has firm, strong roots that go deep into the reservoir of God. And she has the confidence to weather any storm because God is with her, even if sometimes it doesn't always feel like He is there. Our emotions and perspective can be misleading in that way. If we aren't looking for God in our lives, we may never realize the actions He is taking with every step we take. As Janet has learned, walking with the Lord is not about feeling, but about knowing that He is close. He is always with us even if we don't always feel Him—in every step we take, in the darkness of the valleys and in the sunshine of the mountains that we travel in our lives.

CHAPTER 4

When Money Matters—
Overcoming the Loss of Finances

He will fulfill the desire of those who fear Him;
He also will hear their cry and save them.
The LORD preserves all who love Him.

PSALM 145:19-20

THE SOVEREIGN

*And my God shall supply all your need
according to His riches in glory by Christ Jesus.
Now to our God and Father
be glory, forever and ever. Amen.*

PHILIPPIANS 4:19-20

Gatlinburg, Tennessee, is a family-friendly tourist town that
serves as the gateway to the Great Smoky Mountain National Park.
Known for rustic hotels, quaint shops, and popular restaurants, all
surrounded by green-clad hilltops and Smoky Mountain peaks. Few
people take time to trace the back roads; but those who turn onto
Campbell Lead Road, just off the bypass from Pigeon Forge, drive by a
remarkable house sprawled at the end of a sloping, winding drive. It's
a 16,512 square-foot super-chalet, nestled on the side of a mountain
with a three-story living room, offering lofty windows and fabulous
views. It's a massive home, and empty.

It belonged to a middle-aged stock trader who apparently bilked
clients out of millions of dollars in an elaborate Ponzi scheme. Some
say he's the hillbilly version of Bernie Madoff. This man, having lost
everything that can be traced, has swapped his chalet for a cell. The
real losses, however, are those of his victims. One of them, a recently-
widowed woman who worked for years as a secretary in Europe, lost
the bulk of her life savings. "I don't know what my future is going to
be now because I have only enough income to pay my rent," she said.
"Literally, I am living on the charity of friends." Like many others, she

thought her investments were secure and her money was safe; and now it's gone.[12]

The Bible says, "Cast but a glance at riches, and they are gone, for they will surely sprout wings and fly off to the sky like an eagle" (Proverbs 23:5 NIV). We've always known that money had wings. But only in recent years have we begun to compre- hend its wingspan. Our savings can vanish in an instant; and if your plans for retirement have changed for the worse, you're in good company. Millions of people have suffered losses in pension accounts, retirement funds, and investment income.

> It's disheartening when we suffer financial loss.

Others have suffered loss of wealth trying to help children, family, and friends in these distressing times. How many people have drained their savings accounts during prolonged bouts of unemploy- ment or because of catastrophic illness and crippling medical bills?

It's disheartening when we suffer financial loss, and even worse if the losses were preventable had we only done something differently or made better decisions. It takes time to process the anger and anguish we feel when money is lost.

But the Bible doesn't see things exactly as we do. According to Scripture, God's perspective on wealth is the opposite of ours. He's not overly concerned about our storing up treasures on earth, but He's highly concerned that we store up eternal treasures.

The Bible warns that money is as transient as a butterfly. Proverbs 27:24 says that riches are not forever, and Ecclesiastes 5:14 warns that wealth can easily perish through misfortune. Paul warned us not to trust in wealth, which is so uncertain (1 Timothy 6:17), and Jesus said,

---

12   Based on multiple press accounts.

"Do not lay up for yourselves treasures on earth, where moth and rust destroy and where thieves break in and steal" (Matthew 6:19). He wasn't forbidding us from being prudent savers or from planning for the future. He was simply saying our permanent wealth is eternal, but the dollar, pound, and euro aren't. Based on this perspective, let me suggest a three-point formula for handling financial loss.

BE UTTERLY DEPENDENT ON GOD

Financial pressures push us to new levels of faith, forcing us to be utterly dependent on Him. The Bible is filled with promises that God will meet the needs of His children. Psalm 23 says that if the Lord is our Shepherd, we shall not lack. Jesus counseled us to study birds and flowers, for the God who feeds and clothes them will care for us. The psalmist said, "I have been young, and now am old; yet I have not seen the righteous forsaken, nor his descendents begging bread" (Psalm 37:25).

Paul told his readers, "My God shall supply all your need according to His riches in glory by Christ Jesus" (Philippians 4:19). In 2 Corinthians 9:8, the Lord promised that He "is able to make all grace abound toward you, that you, always having all sufficiency in all things, may have an abundance for every good work."

Sometimes financial panic is a gale pushing us onto the shores of God's faithfulness. In 1861, a YMCA convention was held in Carlisle, Pennsylvania, with many Christian business leaders present. Presiding was John Wanamaker, the famous retailer known today as the father of modern advertising. On the second day of the conference, a telegram arrived with shocking news. The banking house of Jay Cook & Company had failed, resulting in terrible losses for Wanamaker and for others at the convention. Soon reports flowed in of other firms failing and of a nationwide financial crash. A feeling of panic swept the convention, making it hard to conduct business or continue the proceedings.

One of the delegates, Erastus Johnson, came across Psalm 61:2: "From the end of the earth I will cry to You, when my heart is overwhelmed; lead me to the rock that is higher than I." Based on that verse, Johnson wrote a song that was instantly put to music at the convention and sung over and over. It became a favorite hymn of its day, and it's still good for us now:

> *Oh! Sometimes the shadows are deep,*
> *And rough seems the path to the goal,*
> *And sorrows, sometimes how they sweep*
> *Like tempests down over my soul.*
>
> *Oh, then to the Rock let me fly*
> *To the Rock that is higher than I.*
> *Oh, then to the Rock let me fly*
> *To the Rock that is higher than I.*

You can stand on the Rock without a penny in your pocket, without a dollar in your account, without a crumb in your pantry. He'll provide in His own time and way, and we can trust Him with all our needs. He who spared not His own Son but freely gave Him for us all, how will He not also give us all things we need?

BE RICH IN GOOD DEEDS

The Bible also tells us to be content with whatever we have, though it be little, and to be rich in good deeds. The words of 1 Timothy 6:6-8 seem to have been written with today's headlines in mind: "Godliness with contentment is great gain. For we brought nothing into this world, and it is certain we can carry nothing out. And having food and clothing, with these we shall be content."

The passage warns about the dangers of loving money too much, then adds: "Command those who are rich in this present age not to be haughty, nor to trust in uncertain riches but in the living God, who gives us richly all things to enjoy. Let them do good, that they be rich in good works, ready to give, willing to share, storing up for them-selves a good foundation for the time to come"(verses 17-19).

What practical advice during a recession: Be content. Enjoy what you have. Be rich in good works.

Job said he came into the world naked and would leave it the same way, and Paul said we brought nothing into the world and will take nothing out. But Jesus said we can lay up treasures in heaven. When we're rich in good deeds, we're making an investment that will never lose its value and that will pay dividends everlastingly. Look around for something you can do for someone else.

BE FOCUSED ON SPIRITUAL WEALTH

Another good Bible study for troubled times is found in Ephesians. In chapters 1-3, the apostle Paul provides an inventory of our endless, everlasting wealth. The words "rich" and "riches" occur six times in these chapters, and all six verses are worth memorizing on the asset side of our mental ledger:

- *In Him we have redemption through His blood, the forgiveness of sins, according to the* riches *of His grace . . .* (Ephesians 1:7)

- ... *the* riches *of the glory of His inheritance in the saints . . .* (Ephesians 1:18)
- *God, who is* rich *in mercy . . .* (Ephesians 2:4)
- *. . . in the ages to come He might show the exceeding* riches *of His grace in His kindness toward us in Christ Jesus . . .* (Ephesians 2:7)
- *. . . the unsearchable riches of Christ . . .* (Ephesians 3:8)
- *. . . that He would grant you, according to the* riches *of His glory, to be strengthened with might through His Spirit in the inner man . . .* (Ephesians 3:16)

In John 14, Jesus said He's preparing a mansion for us in heaven; and Revelation 21-22 describes a diamond city with golden streets, translucent walls, crystal waters, and a glorious throne—our eternal inheritance in Him, for we are heirs of God and co-heirs with Christ. And this inheritance "can never perish, spoil or fade—kept in heaven for you" (1 Peter 1:4 NIV). This is the wealth that "neither moth nor rust destroys and where thieves do not break in and steal" (Matthew 6:20). We can fall asleep at night pondering how rich we are since Jesus came our way.

We can't effectively insure ourselves against financial loss—there are no truly safe investments—and who knows what the future will hold? If the global economy collapses, we'll face a Great Depression that's unimaginable in severity and scope. But nothing depresses our Lord and there's never a run on heaven's banks. He tells us to not let our hearts be troubled, neither let them be afraid.

There's never a run on heaven's banks.

Just depend on Him, be rich in good deeds, turn your thoughts to wealth eternal, and be not dismayed, whatever the circumstances. God will take care of you.

THE SUFFERING

Personal Story—Timm and Margaret Memmel

*W*ith an economy in recession and unemployment at an all-time high, many people's finances are in shambles. Businesses are closing shop, people are losing their homes, and families are struggling to provide for even the most basic needs. God tells us to rely on Him, but can we really trust Him to provide? Would a powerful and sovereign God really take the time to supply our everyday needs? Even through our darkest times of great financial crisis, we can experience the loving provision that only the Father can supply. Meet Timm and Margaret Memmel.

Timm and Margaret owned a successful auto repair business in San Diego, California, for many years. But when tragedy struck our nation through the terrorist attacks of September 11, 2001, the Memmels' business began a decline from which it would not recover. After 9/11, automakers began offering low financing, opening up a new market of car buyers who previously could not get the credit to buy an automobile. With the surge of new vehicles on the road, the number of people who needed auto repairs shrank drastically, and the only people left in the Memmels' area were those who didn't own a car or couldn't afford to fix their vehicle. Without regular business, their repair shop started struggling. They poured more money into the business, hoping it would eventually turn around—all while praying that God would help the situation to improve. Yet, it seemed the more they prayed the worse their finances got. The couple fell into increasing debt. Timm even remembers not having enough gas in his car some mornings to get to work and open the doors for their employees. The pressure to provide their staff with work and a paycheck was overwhelming, and they stopped writing themselves a check to keep from closing the business's doors.

Struggling to keep up with the bills, Margaret, a former grocery store employee, decided to cross union picket lines and go back to work. On her first day, she received several death threats from picketers, angry that she was working at a supermarket. She prayed a lot, and believers from their church and small group also prayed for her. The threats stopped, and God's presence and blessing were evident to her each day. The Lord provided her with long hours of work, keeping the family financially afloat for about six months.

But during this time of blessing, the situation with the auto shop continued to decline. In just a few short years, Timm and Margaret found themselves in a place that they never expected to be—they were going to lose everything. They closed the shop and were forced to sell their house to pay back their lenders, even after their church paid one of their mortgage payments for them. Timm and Margaret were blessed to find realtors who reduced their commission while selling the home so they could save as much money as possible. Their friends and family helped clean the house to prepare it for sale, and packed up the family's things so they didn't have to hire a moving company. The assistance Timm and Margaret received was a constant reminder to them of the Lord's compassion and provision.

As they set off for their cross-country relocation, the couple said goodbye to their grown children, who would not be joining them. Their two daughters, nineteen and twenty-one, moved into apartments in town, while their son, the oldest of the three, moved to Wisconsin to help Margaret's ailing mother. Husband and wife alone moved to Charlotte, North Carolina, to take advantage of the lower cost of living. It was heartbreaking splitting from their family, friends, church, and everything they identified as home—but it was a new adventure. Being on their own again without children to care for and trying to survive financially was reminiscent of when they were newly married.

The couple attempted to make the best out of living in North Carolina, but they desperately wanted to move back to Southern California. Every attempt at moving back was unsuccessful—it seemed they would never return. Timm reflected on the previous years—the time when their business was still healthy—and remembered that he had rededicated his life to Christ only six months before their financial trouble began. Was he being tested . . . or punished? Without a doubt, Timm trusted God and knew He was in control of their lives, but he also desperately wanted to know if he had done something wrong. He was willing to change. As Timm wrestled with these thoughts, Margaret felt paralyzed by the pressures of their situation and did the only thing she knew to do—she turned to the Lord in prayer.

Concluding that God must have put them through these trials for a reason, Timm and Margaret focused on one day at a time. It is not uncommon for financial pressures to cause marriages to break apart and believers to fall away from the Lord, but the couple was committed to being faithful to each other and God. This determination strengthened their marriage and drew them into a deeper relationship with the Lord.

While living on the East Coast, both of their parents' health started failing. Their new location finally proved to be beneficial, as Timm and Margaret were closer to their parents and had more flexibility to visit them and talk with them about the Lord. When Margaret mother's deterioration grew more severe, periodic visits weren't enough anymore and the couple moved to Wisconsin. This allowed them the opportunity to spend quality time with her before she died. Also during their time in Wisconsin, Margaret was presented with the opportunity to share the Gospel with her sister and brother-in-law, bringing them to Christ—a sight Margaret thought she would never see.

Although the Memmels had experienced many blessings during their time in North Carolina and Wisconsin, the pair still missed San Diego, so they attempted to move back. Timm and a friend had always talked about working together, but the details had never panned out. Around the time the couple was trying to get back to the area, Timm's friend started his own company and offered Timm a job—just as they had always planned. Accepting the job, Timm and Margaret moved back to San Diego—finally reunited with their daughters. Their son and his wife, along with a new baby daughter, moved back to San Diego as well. The Memmels were able to buy a house that they love, and Timm is able to provide for them like never before. God not only brought them through their trials—He brought them home and restored their lives.

Now Timm and Margaret are more humble and appreciative of their possessions. Formerly used to having the biggest and best of everything, suddenly all those material things don't seem very important. They have trimmed back to minimize their lifestyle, and have discovered the difference between what they want versus what their needs really are.

God has been faithful through it all—always providing for their essential needs. They have held on to trusting in Him and believe that

He will lead them to the place where He wants them to be, just as He has been doing all along. God never gave them anything they could not handle, and He has now provided more than they could imagine He ever would. There were challenges—and there still will be—but God is on their side, directing them along the path that He desires for them. Had they stayed comfortable in San Diego, perhaps they would not have traveled to see their parents in their last days. Maybe Margaret's sister and her husband would not have become Christians. Nothing can be certain, but it appears the Lord put them in the place they needed to be, when they needed to be there. He led and used them as a tool for His glory as they became God's voice and shared His love to those along their journey.

God has a bigger plan than we may think or realize. He is sovereign and knows a future that we cannot fathom. Obstacles and hardships that we may view as a curse are sometimes blessings in disguise. We are surrounded by these blessings every day—we just need the right perspective to see them clearly.

CHAPTER 5

Medical Cares—Weathering the Loss of Health

My flesh and my heart fail;
but God is the strength of my heart
and my portion forever.

PSALM 73:26

THE SOVEREIGN

Blessed is he who considers the poor;
The LORD will deliver him in time of trouble.
The LORD will preserve him and keep him alive,
And he will be blessed on the earth;
You will not deliver him to the will of his enemies.
The LORD will strengthen him on his bed of illness;
you will sustain him on his sickbed.

PSALM 41:1-3

Missionary Isobel Kuhn wrote a book entitled *In the Arena*, in which she explained how her various adversities and problems had become platforms upon which she could minister and witness for the Lord. Her final chapter involved the loss of her health and her battle with breast cancer. She said that dealing with such a disease absolutely requires a "sound mind," as promised to Christians in 2 Timothy 1:7.

Isobel said her natural impulse was to panic at every moment, imagining complications. If she coughed, she imagined she had lung cancer. If she had a toothache, she feared cancer in the mouth. Every tickle and twinge was instantly interpreted as a grim new enemy. But she kept reminding herself that God has not given us a spirit of fear, but of power and of love and of a sound mind.

Thus she was learning a new lesson, she wrote, "or an old lesson in a new form. I had to refuse to allow my imagination to play with my future. That future, I believe, is ordered of God, and no man can guess it. For me to let myself imagine how or when the end would come was not only unprofitable, it was definitely harmful, so I had to bring my thoughts into captivity that they might not dishonor God."[13]

Isobel discovered it best to stay as busy as she could, given her weakened condition. Though largely confined to bed, she drew up a daily schedule that fit within the limits of her strength: she worked on her book, engaged in a ministry of prayer, read and studied, and rejoiced in letters and cards that came from all over the world.

Sometimes when she wanted to devote herself to prayer, she found she didn't have the strength for it. But she did what she could. "Sound health and a normal life I cannot have while on this platform," she wrote, "therefore I accept the fact and do not fret about it." She enjoyed looking at the flowers that came into her sickroom, visiting with friends and family, and reminding herself that "the platform of a dread disease becomes but a springboard for heaven."

God created Adam and Eve in a state of perfect health, and their bodies were free from disease. When they sinned, the whole order of nature was convulsed; and sickness became a grim reality, death an unavoidable eventuality. At least a portion of our days on earth will be spent sick, ill, diseased, injured, wounded, dying, or dead. The loss of health can come suddenly or slowly. But through it all, God does not give us a spirit of fear, but of power, of love, and of a sound mind. We can't give in to panic or allow ourselves to live in a state of continual depression or fear, for the joy of the Lord is still our strength.

Even in illness and injury, we need to be biblical Christians, claiming God's promises and living with His presence and purposes in mind. It helps us to remember that even the biblical heroes of old weren't immunized against illness. Job suffered terrible prolonged illnesses that

---

13   Isobel Kuhn, *In the Arena* (Singapore: OMF Books, 1960), 225–232.

marred his body and brought constant misery. Paul watched helplessly as his friends Epaphroditus and Trophimus tossed and turned with deadly fever. Hezekiah was struck by terminal illness, and King Asa had a wasting disease in his feet. Peter's mother-in-law occupied a sickbed, Samuel became feeble, and King David anguished over the condition of his newborn. Paul prayed three times to be healed of his illness, his thorn in the flesh. And even the Son of Man suffered violent, life-ending injuries and excruciating pain at the hands of His enemies.

KEEP TRUSTING GOD ANYWAY

Our greatest challenge in the loss of health is to keep trusting God anyway. We know He cares for us, and we know we have ultimate healing through the shed blood and empty tomb of Jesus Christ. But the loss of health affects us emotionally as much as physically. It puts us at risk financially and vocationally. It sets us on a collision course with our most dreaded enemy—death—and we may find ourselves in real mortal danger, exposed to possible suffering, chronic pain, and the loss of all we hold dear in life.

> Our greatest challenge in the loss of health is to keep trusting God anyway.

Perhaps the greatest truth in the entire Bible as it relates to sickness among Christians is John 11:4, when Jesus declared: "This sickness will not end in death. No, it is for God's glory so that God's Son may be glorified through it" (NIV).

He spoke those words after hearing that His friend, Lazarus, was ill. Lazarus was indeed sick, and he did die. By the time Jesus arrived, he'd been in the tomb four days. But Jesus didn't say that Lazarus' sickness wouldn't include death. He said that it wouldn't end in death. It would provide instead an occasion for God to be glorified.

Christians in sickness don't say "10-4" but "11:4," and John 11:4 can be inscribed in the hospital suite or the sickroom of every believer in the world today. Our illness will not end in death; and everything that happens to us will become a platform for the glory of Him who "works all things according to the counsel of His will" (Ephesians 1:11).

WE HAVE TO WORK HARD TO STAY SPIRITUALLY STRONG IN ILLNESS

Because of this, we have to work hard at staying spiritually and emotionally strong during illness. We often need physical therapy, but God is a great spiritual therapist who can help keep us strong of heart even when we're weak of body. Proverbs 18:14 says, "The spirit of a man will sustain him in sickness."

In olden times, Christian publishers commissioned hymnbooks specifically geared for the sick and disabled to help foster this attitude. The great hymnist, J. M. Neale, for example, edited a nineteenth-century volume entitled *The Invalid's Hymn-Book, Being a Selection of Hymns Appropriate to the Sick Room*. It aimed to bolster the spiritual and emotional health of those whose physical health was in decline. One such hymn in Neale's book said:

> *Are thy toils and woes increasing?*
> *Are the Foe's attacks unceasing?*
> *Look with Faith unclouded,*
> *Gaze with eyes unshrouded,*
> *On the Cross!*[14]

14 www.hymnary.org (accessed February 25, 2010).

The apostle Paul spoke along these lines when he said, "Therefore we do not lose heart. Even though our outward man is perishing, yet the inward man is being renewed day by day" (2 Corinthians 4:16). Periods of illness can be times in which we discover new realms of the faithfulness of God, which is why the Victorian preacher, Charles H. Spurgeon, once declared: "I dare say that the greatest earthly blessing that God can give to any of us is health, with the exception of sickness."

GOD CAN USE US IN SICKNESS

We also have to remember that as long as we're in this world, God intends to use us. Our work isn't over until He takes us home. Elisha was still counseling kings in his sickness that would end in his death (2 Kings 13:14). A glance at Christian history tells us that some of the greatest works for God have been done by people battling sickness, illness, disease, or disability.

We have to persevere as best we can, aiming to do the work God has for us each day. "You can't get much done in life if you only work when you feel good," said basketball star Jerry West.

John Pounds is a good example. He was a tall, muscular teenaged laborer at the docks of Portsmouth, England, who slipped and fell from the top of a ship's mast. When workers reached him, he was nothing but a mass of broken bones. For two years he lay in bed as his bones healed crookedly. His pain never ceased. Out of boredom, he began to read the Bible.

At length, John crawled from bed hoping to find something he could do with his life. A shoemaker hired him, and day after day,

John sat at his cobbler's bench, a Bible open on his lap. Soon he was born again.

John ultimately gathered enough money to purchase his own little shoe shop, and one day he developed a pair of surgical boots for his crippled nephew Johnny, whom he had taken in. Soon John was making corrective shoes for other children, and his little cobbler's shop became a miniature children's hospital.

As John's burden for children grew, he began receiving homeless ones, feeding them, teaching them to read, and telling them about the Lord. His shop became known as "The Ragged School," and John would limp around the waterfront, food in his pockets, looking for more children to tend.

During his lifetime, John Pounds rescued five hundred children from despair and led every one of them to Christ. Moreover, his work became so famous that a "Ragged School Movement" swept England, and a series of laws were passed to establish schools for poor children in John's honor. Boys' homes, girls' homes, day schools, and evening schools were started, along with Bible classes in which thousands heard the Gospel.

When John collapsed and died on New Year's Day 1839 while tending to a boy's ulcerated foot, he was buried in a churchyard on High Street. All England mourned, and a monument was erected over his grave, reading: "Thou shalt be blessed, for they could not recompense thee."[15]

His condition became a platform for the glory of God; and John Pounds is a good reminder that God isn't finished with us just because we grow frail or feeble.

15 Robert J. Morgan, *From This Verse* (Nashville: Thomas Nelson Publishers, 1998), entry for August 13.

SICKNESS POINTS US TOWARD HEAVEN

Finally, Christians are practical people who understand that eventually we're going to make it to heaven, and it will likely be via the "valley of the shadow of death." We may not relish the thought, but we're not overly worried. We recall that Jesus interrupted every funeral He attended, and He delighted in healing the sick of the villages He approached. Every story of healing in the Bible is a token of God's ultimate, eternal healing of all our bodily afflictions, which is part of our redemption gained for us by Christ, by whose stripes we are healed.

If heaven is the worst thing that can happen to us, we shouldn't despair.

An old Puritan once said, "Sickness, when sanctified, teaches us four things: The vanity of the world, the vileness of sin, the helplessness of man, and the preciousness of Christ."

If heaven is the worst thing that can happen to us, we shouldn't despair even amid medical emergencies or the loss of health. We have a Great Physician whose own tomb is empty. We have a heavenly home whose doors are open. And we have a sympathetic Savior who never imparts a spirit of fear, but of power, love, and a sound mind.

THE SUFFERING

Personal Story—Dan Desmond

It was another sunny September day in Southern California. Dan Desmond was on a ten-mile hike with his friend Al in the mountains of San Diego County. Setting off at a steady pace, these two men took the word "hike" literally—there was no strolling on this trek up the trails. But as the pair continued on, Dan struggled to keep up. His right leg wasn't working properly. He couldn't pick it up. Finding a large stick on the ground, he began using it as a staff to help him walk. But after about three miles in, crossing streams and trudging through the wilderness, Dan realized he could go no farther.

Knowing something was wrong, Dan told his friend he needed to stop. As they rested for a minute, Dan told Al about his leg and encouraged him to finish the hike. Dan said he would wait and join him on the way down. Al didn't go anywhere. The two stayed in that spot talking for a few hours and then slowly walked back to the car.

This event was a wake-up call. Looking back, there were probably small signs for about a year before this event; but after the hike, the Desmonds sought medical advice. The resulting weeks were filled with examinations and often painful tests to determine what was causing this weakness in Dan's legs. Following a battery of testing, Dan and Gloria met with the doctor for the words that would change their lives.

"You have Lou Gehrig's disease," said the doctor.

Lou Gehrig's disease, known as amyotrophic lateral sclerosis (ALS) is an incurable disease that affects the nerves controlling muscle movement. People with ALS are slowly paralyzed as the condition spreads, weakening and ultimately deadening nerve cells. It usually starts in the limbs and ends with the paralysis of respiratory muscles.

The doctor appeared struck by the Desmonds' lack of response to this tragic diagnosis. So he tried to clarify the situation for them saying "Don't you understand? I said you have ALS. You're dying. You only have two to five years to live."

Dan gently smiled and said, "Don't you understand? You're dying too. We're all dying."

Later on the Desmonds transferred to another health plan and found that the doctor had written in Dan's medical records, "This guy is some kind of minister, and they understand they have the disease, and it doesn't seem to impact them."

After the diagnosis, the disease progressed quickly. Dan started using a cane, and within a few months relied on a walker. About a year later, he was bound to an electric wheelchair.

Dan had always been a man who followed God's plan. He owned a successful dental laboratory, but sold it after he felt that God was leading him to work (for significantly lower pay) at a seminary. When Dan received his master's degree, he was encouraged by his wife to pursue his passion to minister to people. In 1998, Dan opened a counseling ministry to help anyone who walked through the doors, regardless of their ability to pay, advising each person from a Christ-centered and biblical-based position. As the disease progressed, Dan realized that he couldn't continue his full-time counseling practice, and in February of 2009 he resigned, leaving the organization in the hands of a trusted colleague. It was very difficult for Dan to step down and walk away from the ministry he had passionately loved and built from the ground up. It was another casualty of the disease,

another surrender of His will to God's. But God opened new doors
for Dan using his personal experience with ALS; he still does counseling—just differently.

Staff with the ALS Association and a San Diego hospital provides
Dan's number to patients with ALS because many people tend to
become depressed and suicidal after they are diagnosed. Dan talks
with them, and has brought many to the Lord. One of those people
was an aide provided by the VA who came to massage Dan's legs five
days a week to increase blood circulation. With a captive audience at
his feet, Dan ministered to the man, who did not know Christ. He is
now a Christian and his entire family is in church. While Dan had to
surrender his full-time counseling ministry, lives are being touched
because of this disease.

ALS is not an easy condition to deal with. Dan is learning that he
has to surrender the life he was used to living. He has struggled with
learning his physical limits—even simple things like picking up his
Bible if it falls on the floor is beyond his capability today. Dan used
to complete the projects on his wife's "honey-do" list, but now Dan
relies on a group of friends from his Bible study who come over and
do the chores for him. He is learning to surrender more and more of
his strength as God gives him the grace for each day.

When Dan was still using a walker, he decided to build a planter
in his yard with concrete and stones. He loaded his walker with bags
of concrete and began the arduous process. It was slow going as Dan
hobbled, picked up a stone, put it on the walker, shuffled over to the
wall, and stacked it. The long process continued until the concrete
started hardening too quickly.

"Honey," he called for his wife, Gloria, "Come quick, I need some
help. Throw some water on this."

Gloria grabbed the hose and came running to her husband. About ten feet from Dan, she snagged her foot. Dan saw her tripping. He took off running to catch her and save her from injury. Except Dan's legs didn't work anymore. He collapsed to the ground, and watched as Gloria tumbled to the earth.

"Don't move," Dan said. "I'll come get you." Then they realized that Dan couldn't come get her—he couldn't move—and they burst into laughter. Laughter has become part of this journey as well.

Dan, a self-admitted Type A personality, has competed with his pride to slow down. After he crashed and was thrown from his wheelchair while taking out the trash, his doctor told him, "You have to stop being stupid. If you break a bone, we cut your leg off. If it won't heal, we go up further." Dan finally got the message, but has struggled to change his life from Type A to what often feels like Z-minus.

Dan and Gloria believe that God could heal Dan if He chose to, but that is not their prayer. Their prayer is for God's equipping, that God would use Dan and his disease to reach others for Him. Dan has no regrets. He's counseled thousands of people. His life is blessed with four children—one who is already with the Lord, three living in San Diego County, and three grandchildren. His wife is always beside him. He will miss all those things, but will treasure them while he can.

Would he have planned his life differently? Yes. If he were drafting the script instead of God, would he have written it another way? Yes. But this is the script; and with Christian children, a great marriage, and a deep relationship with Jesus Christ, he doesn't regret a step. He has experienced God's providence even in the midst of his pain.

Dan knows that at any moment, God could take him home. "I know what's in the future, but I don't have to live there. I'm going to live today. And when I die, in less than a nanosecond of time, I'm with

God in heaven. That's not too bad. That's a promotion. I'm looking forward to going Home, but I'm sad for the ones I'm leaving behind."

Dan sees his life as climbing up and around a mountain, one side plummeting downward, the other side rocketing up to the sky. He can't spot what is coming around the next bend of the mountain. Wishing at times he knew what was around the corner; Dan recognizes that God will take care of the future. He is mindful of a plaque given to him by his wife. It says: "Jesus will meet you at the corners." Jesus is always walking with Dan, around every turn, through every stream, and around every pothole along the journey. Dan lives for the day because for him—and really, for all of us—there is simply the present and only God knows what tomorrow will bring.

CHAPTER 6

You Against the World—Living Through the Loss of Support

*Since you have purified your souls in obeying the truth
through the Spirit in sincere love of the brethren,
love one another fervently with a pure heart.*

1 PETER 1:22

THE SOVEREIGN

Beloved, let us love one another,
for love is of God; and everyone who loves
is born of God and knows God.

1 JOHN 4:7

The writer is unknown. The letter arrived by e-mail in the office of a friend of mine, a pastor. Though anonymous, it was deeply personal as it said in broken English: "Many times I ask myself, 'Is there a God who cares about human race and has answer to problems?' I have lost hope in this life and tried to kill myself three times but I failed. Can you do me a favor and help in this? Is there any hope after losing my family?"

Loss of family is the hardest to bear, and family rejection is the worst kind of hurt. Whether it's a spouse who stops loving you, a dad who walks out of your life, a mother who wants nothing more to do with you, a sibling from whom you are estranged, or a child who leaves home in anger or prodigality—it's a devastating loss. Divorce is often understood as more painful than death because it involves a choice; somewhere in a divorce, there's usually a level of rejection not seen when a loved one passes away.

The love and support of one's family is the basis of self-worth, mental health, goal setting, and the ability to interact positively with others. The benefits of receiving affirmation are endless. When we lose the support and praise of those we love the most, the pain is tremendous.

The first death in history occurred when Cain and Abel had a falling out. Later in Genesis, the same story is echoed in the rejection of Joseph by his brothers. Many years later, the remorseful brothers were still haunted by their betrayal of Joseph, saying to one another, "We are truly guilty . . . for we saw the anguish in his soul when he pleaded with us, and we would not hear; therefore this distress has come upon us" (Genesis 42:21).

In the story of Job, one of his greatest sorrows was the disagreement with his wife, recorded in chapter 2.

In the story of Jesus, we have several occasions when His family withdrew their understanding and support. John 7:5 says, "For even His brothers did not believe in Him." In Mark 3, they feared He was "out of His mind" (v. 21). Perhaps even more crushing was the total collapse of our Lord's circle of support on the night He was arrested. Judas betrayed Him, Peter denied Him, and all His disciples fled, leaving Him alone. On the cross, even the Heavenly Father turned His back, leading Jesus to cry, "My God, My God, why have You forsaken Me?" (Matthew 27:46)

> When we lose the support and praise of those we love the most, the pain is tremendous.

Our feelings of loss are especially acute if our family resents us because of our faith in Christ. Francis Schaeffer understood what this felt like. Today we remember him as a Christian missionary apologist who challenged a world of skeptics to consider the truths of the Bible. But as a young man, Francis faced hostile parents who fiercely opposed his idea of going into the ministry. They'd always wanted their son to be an engineer. In preparing for Christian service, he so went against their wishes that his mother carried an unforgiving and bitter spirit far into his years of ministry and down into old age.[16]

---

16   L. G. Parkhurst, Jr., *Francis & Edith Schaeffer* (Minneapolis: Bethany House, 1996), 32.

A FATHER WHO LOVES US

If you're feeling a level of family rejection today, remember that you still have a Heavenly Father who loves you. Because Christ was forsaken by God, we need never be. Because He was separated from His Father's love on Calvary, we are united in the Father's love forever. The Apostle Paul prayed that his readers would comprehend "what is the width and length and depth and height" of God's love for us (Ephesians 3:18).

Romans 8 says that nothing in all creation can separate us from His love. Colossians 3 says that our lives are hidden with Christ in God. John 10 says that nothing can ever snatch us out of His hand.

"When my father and my mother forsake me," says Psalm 27:10, "then the Lord will take care of me."

In Isaiah 49:15-16, the Lord said, "Can a woman forget her nursing child, and not have compassion on the son of her womb? Surely they may forget, yet I will not forget you. See, I have inscribed you on the palms of My hands."

> If you're feeling a level of family rejection today, remember that you still have a Heavenly Father who loves you.

Faced with His friends deserting Him on the eve of His crucifixion, Jesus said, "Indeed the hour is coming, yes, now has come, that you will be scattered, each to his own, and will leave Me alone. And yet I am not alone, because the Father is with Me" (John 16:32). It was the Father's presence that strengthened Jesus during His arrest and trial, and the loss of the Father's presence on the cross, as I said, that proved His greatest anguish. But His anguish became our answer.

Echoing the words of Jesus, the apostle Paul said in his last extant paragraph, just prior to his own execution: "At my first defense no one stood with me, but all forsook me . . . but the Lord stood with me and strengthened me" (2 Timothy 4:16-17).

He has promised never to leave us nor forsake us. If we could only understand the depth of God's love for us, much of our loneliness would evaporate like dew in the sunshine.

A BROTHER WHO DIED FOR US

We also have a Brother who died for us. I've already referred to this, for it's a truth that can't be removed from our Father's love. But think of how grateful we should be for our kinship with Jesus Christ. He called us His friends and His brothers, and He said in John 15:13-14, "Greater love has no one than this, than to lay down one's life for his friends. You are My friends. . . ."

When Christiana Tsai, the daughter of a Chinese political leader, announced to her family she had become a Christian, she was engulfed in successive waves of abuse, ridicule, rejection, and persecution. One of her brothers tore up her Bible in front of her. But Christiana later wrote, "I . . . silently looked to God. Suddenly I saw a vision of Christ on the cross, a crown of thorns on His head and with nails in His hands, and I knew He had suffered for my sins, had purchased my head with His crown, and my hands with His nails. Was there anything I couldn't bear for Him who had suffered so much for me?"

Christiana determined to treat her family as graciously as possible, knowing that Christ was beside her, loving and strengthening her. Later one of her older brothers came to her. "Tell me about

Christianity and why you became a Christian," he asked, adding, "I have noticed that in spite of the way we treat you now, you seem much happier than you used to be. I think I would like to believe, too."[17]

The apostle Peter told wives whose faith was rejected by their husbands to display an inner beauty that comes from a gentle spirit. In so doing, they may win their husbands to Christ "without a word" (1 Peter 3:1-6).

The Bible tells us to live peaceably with everyone, "if it is possible, as much as depends on you" (Romans 12:18).

When we lean on the strength of our elder Brother, walking in His steps, resting in His love, and devoted to His cause, we'll find that He can actively work in painful situations, and He can give us a gracious spirit. The loss of family support can be turned to gain as He works all things together for our good (Romans 8:28).

A COMFORTER WHO WALKS WITH US

We have a third pillar of support—a Comforter who walks with us. In the Upper Room Discourse of John 13-17, Jesus told His disciples that though He was leaving them, He was not abandoning them. "It is to your advantage that I go away," He said in John 16:7.

That's a remarkable statement—it's to our *advantage* that Jesus leave us, leave the world? It's *better* for us that He's gone?

Yes, Jesus said. "It is to your advantage that I go away; for if I do not go away, the Helper (Comforter) will not come to you; but if I depart, I will send Him to you."

Jesus, having taken on the form of a servant and become a human being at His birth in Bethlehem, was localized. He has no clone, and

---

17   Christiana Tsai, *Queen of the Dark Chamber* (Chicago: Moody Press, 1954), 72–73.

He is limited in His humanity to being in one place at one time. By His Spirit, however, He can be with all of us simultaneously.

That's our ultimate reservoir of grace. It's the Holy Spirit of Christ who lives within us, through whom our Lord lives in our hearts, minds, and very bodies. It's the Holy Spirit who fills us with boldness to speak the Word. It's the Holy Spirit who produces within us the fruits of love, joy, peace, patience, kindness, gentleness, and self-control. It's the Holy Spirit who brings to mind the Word of God and helps us recall needed promises at critical moments. It's the Holy Spirit who illumines our minds as we study the Bible so that God's Word burns within our hearts. It's the Holy Spirit who serves as a deposit within us, guaranteeing our eternal inheritance. And it's the Holy Spirit who ministers to our spirits, reassuring us that we are God's children.

None of this is lost when we're rejected by loved ones. In fact, the Comforter becomes ever sweeter and His comforts ever more precious.

A FAMILY WHO BELONGS TO US

Finally, we also have a family who belongs to us, and to whom we belong—the church. The fellowship of Christians is the Body of Christ and the family of God. When Jesus felt rejected by kin, He said that His real brothers and sisters were "whoever does the will of God" (Mark 3:35). He had more affinity with His followers who believed in Him than with His own family who didn't. Sometimes we find our greatest support, love, friendship, and fellowship with God's people in our Christian friendships, small groups, and church gatherings.

Whenever we feel lonely or rejected, we must guard against withdrawing into isolationism. We can't be hermits. We have to reach out in love, finding someone to serve, seeking a kindness to do. The Bible says that a person who has friends must show himself friendly (Proverbs 18:24, KJV).

So to answer the question at the beginning of this chapter—Is there any hope after losing one's family?—the answer is yes, there is. We have a Savior who is the God of hope. When we have the love of a Father, the support of a Brother, the presence of a Comforter, and the availability of the Family of God, there's more than hope.

There's victory.

THE SUFFERING

Personal Story—Sohrab Ramtin

We grow up with an innate connection to our home: our family, friends, and mentors, the place we live, the food we eat, the stories we grow up reading. It is impossible to remove a person from those memories and their culture. We live in a global society, but on a basic level each person is still connected to their roots. What if the culture you grew up in was at odds with your beliefs? What if following God meant giving up the society around you and experiencing rejection by those closest to you? For some Christians, these are not rhetorical questions, they are reality. In regions around the world, believers are persecuted for their faith; and even in the face of adversity, under the threat of death, they are living their faith nonetheless.

Meet Sohrab Ramtin. . . .

Pastor Sohrab Ramtin, a former Muslim, has been rejected by his native country of Iran, and has been labeled a threat by the Iranian government. He knows many who have experienced rejection by their parents, siblings, and spouses for their faith. Today Sohrab pastors two Iranian Christian churches in San Diego County, reaching out to Farsi-speaking peoples (primarily Iranians and Afghans) to share the Gospel with Muslims. He also conducts a television and radio broadcast ministry that sends the Gospel into Iran and Afghanistan by satellite.

Sohrab was born in Iran and grew up Muslim before the Islamic Revolution in 1979, when its monarchy was replaced with the current

Islamic Republic. The child of a journalist, his parents were open-minded—allowing Sohrab to read many books. As a devout Muslim, one of the books he read most faithfully was the Koran. Sohrab practiced his faith, religiously doing his prayers while desiring a deep, personal relationship with God. Yet he was left feeling empty—guilty for the sin he committed and desperate to rid himself of the burden of sin that was weighing him down. Determined to rid himself of his affliction, Sohrab committed himself to more prayer and a devout life. But no matter how hard he tried, the shame could not be lifted. One glimmer of hope came as he read about Moses and Jesus in the Koran. Intrigued to know more about these great men, he decided to turn to the Bible for answers.

When he expressed this interest in the Bible to friends and a teacher, they told him not to touch the book—that Christians and Jews had changed the Bible, removing any mention of Mohammed. But Sohrab could not be dissuaded, and his desire was fulfilled when his father brought home a Farsi translation of the Bible. Sohrab was amazed at the coincidence, because he had never shared his interest in reading the Bible with his father. (Of course today he recognizes that it was no coincidence that his father brought a Bible home—it was God at work in his life!) So, at fourteen years of age, Sohrab opened the pages of Scripture for the first time, struggling to understand the truths hidden in the pages. The Farsi translation was formal, equivalent to an English-speaking teenager trying to read the King James Version. He grew lost trying to grasp the Bible's stories, until he came to the Psalms and fell in love with God's Word. The Psalmist's personal, open prayers and expression of intimate thoughts of God were unlike any prayers Sohrab had ever experienced through the repetitious Islamic creeds.

Not long after this experience—at the conclusion of the Islamic Revolution in 1979, Sohrab and his family moved to the United States, where he enrolled in a university. One of his professors, a Christian, reached out to Sohrab and explained the Gospel to him. When Sohrab finally understood Jesus—who He was and what He had done, he was amazed. He had been thirsty for years, desperately craving a personal relationship with God, and Jesus was a fountain of fresh water that he had finally found after walking through a dry, empty desert. After accepting Christ, Sohrab continued his education, including his studies to become a pastor. During this time, he shared the Gospel with his parents who, years later, both came to know the Lord as well.

Sohrab recognizes that he was blessed to have such accepting parents and to have the opportunity to live in the United States with the freedom to choose and pursue his faith. But he ministers to many people who have experienced the very personal loss of their family's support. One Iranian woman who came to the Lord suffers continual persecution by her strong Muslim family. Her husband was a member of the Revolutionary Guard, the controversial military branch commonly used to suppress dissenters. Sohrab is committed to encouraging this woman as she suffers and prays for her family's salvation.

Suffering is very real for many Christians in Islamic countries. If a Muslim leaves Islam, they are considered apostate, and many countries, like Iran, sanction their murder. One man, fearing for his life because he accepted Christ, fled from Iran to Iraq. He is still in constant danger and maintains a low profile because there are still agents from the Iranian government trying to locate him. The murder of Muslims who have left their faith is not practiced regularly, but persecution is an everyday occurrence for many. They know that making the choice to follow Jesus could cause them to lose their family, jobs, and even their lives, yet they do it willingly.

In an ideal situation, the church then becomes a person's family after they have been rejected. But so many churches in Iran are greatly persecuted and under intense surveillance by the government. Believers in these countries remain disconnected from one another because of the danger in identifying themselves as Christians. Sohrab even refuses to connect Christians in Iran and Afghanistan because of the danger that someone could be a spy and alert the authorities.

Even from outside his home country, Sohrab experiences persecution for his ministry to the Muslim people, whom he loves. He has been insulted and even threatened with his life. Because of his broadcasts, he was featured in a video created and circulated by the Iranian government, labeling him as an "Agent of U.S. Imperialism." There is no freedom of religion in Iran—Christians, Jews, Baha'i, and even Muslims are persecuted. The government is especially threatened by the message of the Gospel. Muslims are recognizing the truth of Christ when they hear it. This has led the country to turn their back on Sohrab. He misses the Iran of his childhood and the culture in which he was raised. But these desires do not compare to his faith in Jesus Christ. He is proud to follow Christ and has found comfort within the community of his congregation.

Because of his personal experiences, Sohrab is able to tell Muslims that suffering is a part of being a Christian. Followers of Christ must be willing to take up their cross and endure persecution because they will face hardship and rejection by their family or peers, especially in Muslim-controlled countries. The Gospel cannot be separated from suffering. There will eventually be a place where there will be no more persecution and suffering, but it is not on this earth. Even in the face of suffering, these Muslims are hearing the truth, recognizing it, and accepting the personal relationship with God.

After one man in Iran contacted Sohrab by phone, the Iranian Intelligence Ministry, who monitored the call, arrested the man and took him to their headquarters. They threatened him and told him to stop contacting Christian organizations outside the country or they would "take care of him." He told them, "I don't care. You can do whatever you want to. I have found the truth. I have life in Jesus. Even if you kill me, I'm not going to give up on that."

The truth of the Gospel is a powerful, life-changing message. The Shepherd is calling His people, and they are responding to Him no matter who or what stands in their way. Just as these Christians know, believing in Jesus can cost an enormous price. But they are also finding out that the cost is worth the reward of the eternal life and great love that God gives to those who accept Him. Our family, friends, and government may all turn their backs on us, but even in the midst of our distress, God is there to comfort and provide all that we need.

CHAPTER 7

The Pink Slip—Moving Forward After the Loss of Your Job

Oh, fear the LORD, you His saints!
There is no want to those who fear Him.
The young lions lack and suffer hunger;
but those who seek the LORD
shall not lack any good thing.

PSALM 34:9-10

THE SOVEREIGN

Surely goodness and mercy
shall follow me all the days of my life;
and I will dwell in the house
of the LORD forever.

PSALM 23:6

No one knows who coined the phrase "pink slip," but it seems to date to the turn of the twentieth century, when many employees were still paid in cash. Each week's wages came in an envelope, and anyone being laid off that week would find a notice—usually on pink paper—in the envelope along with the final wages. The earliest reference to the phrase is dated by *Random House Dictionary* as 1910, so it's been part of our language for more than one hundred years.[18]

Few people today get an actual pink slip, but millions have been pink-slipped recently. Economists say that employment is a "lagging" indicator of the economy, one of the last things to improve during a recovery. But to those who have lost their jobs, it's far more than a "lagging indicator." It is a blow in the stomach.

Millions have been pink-slipped recently.

Many people spend their childhood planning what they want to do when they "grow up." Throughout school, counseling occurs to determine what vocation best fits students' skills and interests. Many people find their identity

18   Frank J. Prial, "Among Those Let Go, the Pink Slip Itself." *The New York Times*, http://www.nytimes.com/1991/06/18/nyregion/among-those-let-go-the-pink-slip-itself.html, accessed February 26, 2010.

in their vocation—I'm a doctor, a sales rep, a homemaker, a teacher, a landscaper, a builder. We move heaven and earth to track down prospective employers and excel in interviews. We rejoice when a job opens up, and we spend the best hours of our waking week on the job. We develop friendships with coworkers, contacts with our customers and clients; and we pay our bills and support our lifestyles with the wages we earn. We depend on benefits to sustain our insurance and retirement plans.

> Pink slips bring with them a sense of rejection.

In a pink flash, all that can vanish; and pink slips bring with them a sense of rejection, a drain on our self-image, and a feeling of embarrassment or frustration over our misfortune. We suffer mental anguish as well as economic distress. Our family's well-being is put in jeopardy, and our marriages can suffer strain.

People who lose their jobs often have difficulty waking up and starting the day. They feel aimless and sometimes suffer a loss of ambition and a fear they'll never find another job. Fatigue and irritability plague them, and they sometimes go through stages of grief akin to the death of a loved one.

Nothing prepares you for the words: "It just isn't working out. We appreciate your efforts, but we'll have to let you go."

One woman, an aspiring writer who landed a job at a Canadian newspaper, heard those very words, and they hit her like a cold wave. "Suddenly," she recalled, "I realized beyond the loss of income, that I would no longer see my co-workers. I would lose my routine. It felt as if I had failed. . . . My eyes started to well up with tears. I thought I could put on a brave face, but the drops broke through into streams on my cheeks. I turned into a blubbering child in a matter of seconds."

"We'll let you collect yourself in here," said her boss kindly, giving her a warm hug. About five minutes later, recalls the employee, "I gathered the shattered bits of my pride and worked for the rest of the afternoon." Since then, she's been bumming around at her parents' house, trying to figure out what went wrong.[19]

GOD KNEW IT IN ADVANCE

In trying to figure it out, we begin by remembering that God is in charge. He is still on the Throne, and He knew in advance what would happen. Dr. A. W. Tozer wrote, "To the child of God, there is no such thing as an accident. He travels an appointed way."[20]

Psalm 37:23 says, "The steps of a good man are ordered by the Lord, and He delights in his way." It's pointed out that if our *steps* are ordered by the Lord, so are our *stops*. "My times are in Your hand," said David in Psalm 31:15, and this from a man who was not only fired by his "boss," but who was pursued by his former employer in a deadly game of cat-and-mouse in the wilderness. But it was comforting to David in Psalm 139 to remember that God knew his sitting down and his rising up; He comprehended his path; He was acquainted with all his ways. "You have hedged me behind and before. . . And in Your book they were all written, the days fashioned for me, when as yet there were none of them. How precious also are Your thoughts to me, O God!"

If you've lost your job, it doesn't mean you have to lose your joy. Remember that God knows all about it; He anticipated it, He has reasons for it, He cares, and He still rules and overrules.

---

19 Jennifer Tan, "Losing Your Job and Keeping Your Dignity," *Power to Change*, http://www.iamnext.com/career/ lostjob.html, accessed February 26, 2010.
20 A. W. Tozer, *We Travel An Appointed Way* (Camp Hill, PA: Christian Publications, May 1988), 3.

HE GUIDES US

This is also a good time to review the "guidance verses" of the Bible. Remember that Proverbs 3:5-6 promises as we trust the Lord with all our hearts and acknowledge Him in all our ways, He will guide us in all our paths. Psalm 23 says our Shepherd will lead us in the right paths. Isaiah wrote, "Thus says the Lord. . . . I am the Lord your God, who teaches you to profit, who leads you by the way you should go" (Isaiah 48:17).

That's an employment-friendly verse if I've ever heard of one.

I'd also like to remind you of a scene in the Book of Numbers. In chapter 9, God's guidance among the children of Israel took visible form in the mysterious cloud, which at night turned to fire. Whenever this cloud lifted from above the tent, the Israelites set out; whenever it settled, the Israelites camped. When the cloud remained over the tabernacle a long time, the Israelites obeyed the Lord's order and did not set out. Sometimes the cloud was over the tabernacle only a few days; sometimes only one night; sometimes a year. But whether by day or by night, whenever the cloud lifted, they set out.

We no longer have His visible cloud above us, for we have His invisible Spirit within us and His infallible Word in our hands. We have His providential ordering of our circumstances, and His promise to direct us in all our ways. If we seem "stuck" for the moment, even if it appears to be for a prolonged period, we're better off to remain stuck in God's will than to wander off on our own. Sometimes we can make a lot of progress when we're standing still, though it doesn't appear so at the time. If as best you can determine, you're in God's will, try not to worry about the pace of things. Just take one day at a time, do your best, and let Him lead your step by His divine agenda. The Lord knows the way through the wilderness.

SELF-PITY IS A TRAP

Along the way, guard vigilantly against self-pity. There's an emotional equation in life that cannot be violated. Whenever we feel wronged or hurt, if we start feeling sorry for ourselves, we'll descend into depression. Psychologists say that while brief flashes of self-pity are normal, this is a particularly self-sustaining attitude. Children who are teased or hurt at school can still be nursing their wounds and suffering ill effects as adults. It arises from a wounded ego and results in a sense of worthlessness.

Guard vigilantly against self-pity.

That's not the way God intends for His children to feel. Whatever happens, don't give up. Pick yourself up. Give yourself a talking to. Preach yourself a sermon. Get some exercise. Get up and stay busy. Don't sit in front of the television with a bag of potato chips. Maybe you've had the breath knocked out of you; but as soon as possible, get your heart pumping again and your lungs breathing.

TAKE THE NEXT LOGICAL STEP BY FAITH

In his book, *The Red Sea Rules,* Rob Morgan points out that on the shores of the Red Sea, the Israelites couldn't see into the distance. They had no binoculars that could view Canaan, nor even the opposite shore. But the Lord gave them a simple plan: *Tell the children of Israel to go forward.*

The old commentator, C. H. Mackintosh, had an interesting view about this. He believed the Red Sea did not divide throughout all at once, but opened progressively as Israel moved forward, so that they needed to trust God for each fresh step. Mackintosh wrote: "God never gives guidance for two steps at a time. I must take one step, and then I get light for the next. This keeps the heart in abiding dependence upon God."

When the communists overran China, missionary Isobel Kuhn escaped on foot with her young son, Danny, across the dangerous, snow-covered Pienma Pass. She finally arrived at Myitkyina in Upper Burma, but there she was stranded "at the world's end" without money, unable to speak the language, and still half a globe away from home. "I cannot tell you the dismay and alarm that filled me," she later wrote.

But in her perplexity, she made two decisions. "The first thing is to cast out fear," she said. "The only fear a Christian should entertain is the fear of sin. All other fears are from Satan, sent to confuse and weaken us. How often the Lord reiterated to His disciples, 'Be not afraid!'" So Isabel knelt and spread her heart before Him. "I refused to be afraid and asked Him to cast such fears out of my heart."

Trust God for guidance in small increments.

Her second determination was to "seek light for the next step." She had no idea how to get out of Asia; but with God's help, she could figure out what to do that day to provide food and funds, to find a safe place to stay, to find a means of communicating with the outside world.

In time, she arrived back home, safe and sound; but it came by trusting God for guidance in small increments, taking the journey one footprint at a time.

The same strategy works when you're unemployed. When you don't know what to do next, cast out fear and seek light for the next step. Trust God for guidance in small increments; and if you can't see what lies dimly in the distance, do what lies clearly at hand.

Just because you've lost your job doesn't mean God has lost His. He's still on His throne, and He's employed on our behalf. Spread your concerns before Him, get up and going, and trust Him to guide you at every step. "Remember the Lord your God, for it is He who gives you the power to get wealth" (Deuteronomy 8:18).

He will make a way for you.

THE SUFFERING

Personal Story—Mark and Rebecca Gray

*C*areers, jobs, our work—they are a significant part of who we are and often even help to define us. In many ways we have a natural desire to work at something—taking pride in what we've done and feeling accomplished. Providing for ourselves and our families is a tremendous responsibility that requires effort, and often gives us a feeling of satisfaction. So what if that was all stripped away? What if you could no longer provide for yourself and your family? What if the career you had worked decades to establish was suddenly taken from you?

Meet Mark Gray.

Early in his life, Mark planned to one day work in missionary aviation and attended a private Christian college to study the field. But his life flew on a different trajectory when he took a part-time weekend job for a small, start-up biotech company in San Diego's rural East County. Mark started as a ranch hand, working with animals and drawing their blood. It was a way to earn extra cash while he studied and flew. But as time went on, he began moving up within the company. In the beginning he worked in the lab: washing glassware, preparing materials, and purifying antibodies in the blood, which were refined and made into diagnostic tests for humans. But by his senior year of college in 1982, the owner offered Mark a two-year position as project manager. At the time Mark was engaged to a young woman named Rebecca, and the job opportunity bought them a few years to determine what they should be doing and where God wanted them to be.

Two years turned into thirty.

Mark had started with the business in its infancy, working out of a lab in his boss's garage with only a few people. Over the years, the company grew, requiring new buildings and more employees and is now one of the ten largest biotech companies in San Diego county with more than six hundred employees. The customer base grew internationally; and what began as a few products ultimately grew to more than 1,500.

With such an invested history with the company, Mark was extremely dedicated to his career as a member of the senior management team. In October 2009, he celebrated his thirtieth year with the company—committed to his work and the continued growth of the business. Everything seemed on track for Mark to remain with the company until retirement.

Just a week after Mark celebrated his thirty years of service with the company, the pink slip came. He was being let go. The explanation? The company was going in a new direction—changing strategies—and Mark wasn't part of the vision. Shocked by the news, Mark and Rebecca were thrust into a sense of uncertainty. The career path they had projected until Mark's retirement had just taken a wild bend through unfamiliar territory. They were paralyzed by the news—never expecting to deal with this in their lives and struggling with the "why" of it all. Mark's job had always been there, but now it was gone.

Having always been a typical, dedicated working man, Mark loved his profession and willingly labored long hours. Being a project manager was not just a job to him, it was an integral part of his life, a deep-rooted definition of his being. When he lost it, he didn't just lose a way to stay busy, a simple task to perform each day—he lost a sense of his own worth and value. His sense of identity was bound to his success; but he also worried about how others would now perceive him as a person. He had always been so confident in his future and his sense of worth, but now found himself traumatized by the loss of something that had been a central part of him.

And while Mark and Rebecca wondered about what others would think, they couldn't help but contemplate the reaction of their children. With three children, they had obvious expenses, as well as tuition to both a private high school and university. How could they tell their children . . . especially their daughter who was away at the time?

Rebecca recalls the dilemma in telling their oldest daughter over an Internet video chat, "That's not the way you to want share that kind of news, but that's what we had to do."

Mark and Rebecca made it through some of the initial, difficult steps, but now deeper questions set in. Having both been Christians since they were young, they turned to God with their questions. They spent a lot of time crying together and praying. Mark remembers asking God, "Why me? Why this? Why now? Why would this happen after thirty years of working so hard?" Yet throughout their uncertainty, Rebecca clung to the belief that even though they did not understand why this was happening, God was still in control. Now they just needed to seek God for what was next in their lives—pursuing His help and assurance for the journey. Little did they know God had a plan in place—He had already provided for their family.

Mark and Rebecca had decided the previous July to lead a boarding house for international students who attended the same private high school as their daughter. Rebecca remembers laughing at the idea of becoming house parents when it was first suggested to her. They had lived in their home for almost twenty-five years of their twenty-seven-year marriage, had watched their kids grow up there, and loved their home. She mostly dismissed the idea, but God had planted a little seed in her heart.

When Rebecca brought up the idea with Mark, he was immediately excited about the opportunity to provide for and minister to the teenagers who would be living in the house. The couple asked their children about it, and received enthusiastic approval of the idea. At the time, they had no idea about the storm looming just a few months ahead. They felt God's calling and listened—taking a step of faith to do something different and embark on a new adventure.

When October came and they lost their biggest source of income, the ministry as house parents revealed itself to be God's provision. The Grays were supplied with room and board, which was not a concern of theirs at the time they accepted the position, but what a blessing it turned out to be. They were astounded and thankful that God had helped their family long before they ever thought they needed it. And since losing his job, Mark has been able to spend more time taking care of the four active teenagers living in the house, plus two of his own children, which would not have been possible if he were still working with his biotech company.

Mark and Rebecca have experienced hardships in the wake of their loss, but say they would not change a thing.

"We're excited to be on this incredible journey with the God of the Universe," Mark now confides. "God wanted to teach me that I can't hold on to things so tightly. I have to be willing to give up and be stripped of what I felt defined me as a person. God is teaching us to trust Him step by step. We know He has a plan."

With a faltering economy and soaring unemployment rates, many are experiencing the same hardships and emotions: stress, worry, defeat, and loss of self-worth. Today, long-time employees are being laid off by their companies, single parents are struggling to keep up with multiple jobs to provide for their children, young people are trying to take their first step into a career when many employers are not hiring, and older generations that expected to retire are instead forced to go back to work. Does this sound far too familiar? Have you experienced the disappointment and pain of losing a job or the stress of trying to make ends meet? God has something to say to you.

CHAPTER 8

Life Is a Disaster—Surviving the Loss of Possessions

Do not sorrow, for the joy
of the LORD is your strength.

NEHEMIAH 8:10

THE SOVEREIGN

He has given food to those who fear Him;
He will ever be mindful of His covenant.

PSALM 111:5

Henry Romersa loved his 1932 Packard Super Eight roadster. It was the same age he was (seventy-seven years old), and he'd salvaged it from an Alabama junkyard in 1961. During Prohibition days, the car had been used as a whiskey runner, and Henry even met the old welder who'd attached the whiskey tank to the car's chassis years before. Henry's classic Packard was one of the delights of his life; and over the decades, he had restored it to mint condition. Though its worth was upwards to $200,000, it was truly irreplaceable.

One day earlier this year, Henry was working on the car in the garage of a home he owned in Nashville. The Packard had been sitting there through the winter, and evidently ethanol in the gasoline had eaten into a fuel line. Unknown to Henry, gasoline was seeping from the car, pooling on the garage floor, and drenching the car's cover, lying to one side. When Henry turned the ignition, the car backfired and ignited the gasoline.

Flames shot everywhere: the covering, the floor, the car, and the garage. Henry managed to escape the inferno with only singes, minor burns, and some smoke in his lungs. But the car was destroyed, along with the garage and another classic car. Henry still wakes up in the night, grieving his loss. "It was one of only seven in the world," he said, "and now there are only six. I had something very special in my life, a work of art, an irreplaceable thing of beauty. I still wake up at night saying to myself, 'If only I'd been more careful . . . if only I'd taken a few extra moments to pull the covering further away . . . if only I'd checked the fuel lines first. . . ."

But no "if onlys" will bring back the Packard.

"I've learned a great lesson," he said. "I don't really feel I'm much of a people person. Despite a lifetime in higher education and fifty years teaching music in universities, I've not taken time for people as I should have. Students would come by to see me while I was working on a car, and I'd be on my back on the floor beneath the vehicle. All they could see were my feet. And I didn't really want to take time for them, so I'd just keep working. I'm going to do better with that. When you lose something material, even if it's priceless, you learn to focus on the things that are even more important and on things that are eternal."

Those are biblical sentiments. One day when Jesus was speaking, a man in the crowd said, "Teacher, tell my brother to divide the inheritance with me." But Jesus replied, "Take heed and beware of covetousness, for one's life does not consist in the abundance of the things he possesses." Jesus went on to tell about a rich man who kept building larger and larger barns for his crops, but God said to him, "Fool! This night your soul will be required of you; then whose will those things be which you have provided?" Then Jesus added, "So is he who lays up treasure for himself, and is not rich toward God." (See Luke 12:13-21.)

Most of us know and believe our Lord's philosophy on this subject. We shouldn't covet. We should be content and satisfied in life. We shouldn't worry too much about accumulating lots of transient things. We must focus on the eternal and be rich toward God.

Nevertheless we are three-dimensional human beings on a physical planet who need "things" every day. We need clothes to wear, food to eat, cars to drive, houses to shelter us, chairs to sit in, beds to sleep in, pictures to enjoy, and sentimental objects to remind us of precious memories.

Over time, many of us accumulate quite an abundance of things, from diamond rings to priceless cars to irreplaceable photographs. It's a cruel blow when those things slip from our grasp. How many people have grieved over the loss of a billfold or a piece of jewelry? How many have lost homes in fires, floods, mudslides, and earthquakes? How many have been robbed of something precious? How many have seen possessions repossessed and sold at auction? How many have been forced to divest themselves of cherished items when moving into smaller quarters, especially in the sunset years?

The key to recovering from this kind of heartache is to *Let God*.

LET GOD COMFORT YOU

First, let God comfort you. In time of loss, our greatest need is immediate and effective comfort. When Job suffered the loss of all he had, his three friends came "to comfort him" (Job 2:11). They failed their task, for they tried to comfort him with "empty words" (Job 21:34). Job finally muttered in disgust, "Miserable comforters are you all!" (Job 16:2). In the end, only God could comfort him by teaching him valuable lessons, deepening his faith, and restoring in His own way the things Job had lost.

The psalmist expressed praise in Psalm 71 for having a God who comforted him "on every side." He said in Psalm 94:19, "In the multitude of my anxieties within me, Your comforts delight my soul." In Psalm 119:50, we read, "This is my comfort in my affliction, for Your word has given me life."

Speaking to exiles and refugees who had lost not only their homes but their very nation, the Lord said in Isaiah 51:12, "I, even I, am He who comforts you."

The Holy Spirit is called the Comforter in John's Gospel. And the apostle Paul described our Lord as the "God of all comfort" and as One who "comforts the downcast" (2 Corinthians 1:3; 7:6). It's for this reason the Bible tells us to "be of good comfort" (2 Corinthians 13:11).

If you've lost something over which you're distressed, this might be a good time to go to the concordance at the back of your Bible (or online) and look up all 112 references in the Bible to the word *comfort*. If out of our loss we discover the comforting ministry of the God of all comfort, we will gain great treasure.

LET GOD RESTORE YOU

Second, let God restore you. In the book of the ancient prophet Joel, the Lord told the people who had lost their crops, "I will repay you for the years the locusts have eaten. . . . You will have plenty to eat, until you are full, and you will praise the name of the Lord your God, who has worked wonders for you" (Joel 2:25-26 NIV).

We often find that times of great loss are times of great lessons if we can only persevere by faith. William Carey, the "father of modern missions," wanted to translate the Bible into as many Indian languages as possible. He established a large print shop in Serampore where translation work was continually being done.

Carey was away from Serampore on March 11, 1812. His associate, William Ward, was working late. Suddenly Ward's throat tightened and he smelled smoke. He leaped up to discover clouds belching from the printing room. He screamed for help, and workers passed water from the nearby river until 2 a.m., but everything was destroyed.

On March 12, 1812, missionary Joshua Marshman entered a Calcutta classroom where Carey was teaching. "I can think of no easy way to break the news," he said. "The print shop burned to the ground last night." Gone were Carey's massive polyglot dictionary, two grammar books, and whole versions of the Bible. Gone were sets of type for 14 eastern languages, 1,200 reams of paper, 55,000 printed sheets, and 30 pages of his Bengal dictionary. Gone was his complete library. "The work of years—gone in a moment," he whispered.

He took little time to mourn. "The loss is heavy," he wrote, "but as traveling a road the second time is usually done with greater ease and certainty than the first time, so I trust the work will lose nothing of real value. We are not discouraged; indeed the work is already begun again in every language. We are cast down but not in despair."

When news of the fire reached England, it catapulted Carey to instant fame. Thousands of pounds were raised for the work, and volunteers offered to help. The enterprise was rebuilt and enlarged. By 1832, complete Bibles, New Testaments, or separate books of Scripture had issued from the printing press in forty-four languages and dialects. The secret of Carey's success is found in his resiliency. "There are grave difficulties on every hand," he once wrote, "and more are looming ahead. Therefore we must go forward."[21]

LET GOD CHANNEL HIS COMFORT THROUGH YOU

Finally, in times of loss, we enter an opportunity in which we can become more helpful to other people. The Book of 2 Corinthians, in which Paul described the hardships of his work, opens with these words: "Blessed be the God and Father of our Lord Jesus Christ, the Father of mercies and God of all comfort, who comforts us in all

---

21   Robert J. Morgan, *On This Day* (Nashville: Thomas Nelson, 1997), entry for March 12.

our tribulation, that we may be able to comfort those who are in any trouble, with the comfort with which we ourselves are comforted by God" (2 Corinthians 1:2-4).

Richard Wurmbrand is a good example. In his book, *Tortured for Christ*, he tells of being in and out of Communist prisons because of persecution. Despite the loss of possessions and freedom, the principle of tithing was so internalized in his heart and in those of his fellow prisoners that when they received a slice of bread a week and dirty soup every day, they faithfully tithed from it. Every tenth day they gave their soup to weaker brothers, and every tenth week they took their slice of bread and gave it to fellow prisoners in Jesus' name.[22]

We can all do the same. When disaster strikes, we grieve over the loss of things once held dear. But upon deeper, prayerful reflection, we eventually come to realize we can't take any of these "things" with us to heaven; all will perish in the final conflagration at the end of the ages. But the God of comfort can strengthen our hearts, provide our needs, and use us for His glory. Those are treasures that can never perish, and we can strengthen ourselves in His peace, His provision, His presence, and His promises.

He is the God of all comfort.

---

22   Richard Wurmbrand, *Tortured for Christ* (Bartlesville, OK: Living Sacrifice Book Company, 1967), 45.

THE SUFFERING

Personal Story—Heidi Pullen

*I*t was a beautiful October day in sunny California. It was warm; the sun was shining—a typical gorgeous fall day in San Diego County. There was no hint of what the day might bring to thousands of residents on that Sunday morning. By the end of the day a long line of cars crawled bumper to bumper down the one-lane highway, desperately trying to escape the scarlet glow cresting the ridges around the vehicles. The sky was black with smoke and ash. Cell phone service was out, and thousands were virtually stranded on their slow exodus from the furious wildfire. This was the only way out of Ramona, a rural community about thirty-five miles northeast of downtown San Diego. Heidi Pullen was in the thick of it, sitting in her car—along with some clothes, meaningful belongings, and her cat and rabbit. It was slow going—only moving half a block in two hours. As she drove in the opposite direction from her house, the thought crossed her mind that she may never see her home again.

Meet Heidi Pullen.

Heidi was leaving church that Sunday morning in October of 2007 when she received a call from her landlord telling her to hurry home. Heidi lived on a ranch—the same property as her landlord's large log cabin—and loved her home. It was a pretty place in the country, quiet and peaceful. It was also close to her work at Young Life Oakbridge Camp and Conference Center, a Christian camp that facilitates activities and conferences for many ministries, including Young Life—an outreach to lost teens. Driving home, Heidi noticed the enormous plume of smoke off in the distance, and her stomach dropped with the realization that the smoke was very close to Oakbridge and her home. She headed to the camp to see if she could assist with the evacuation of about 150 men who were on a weekend retreat. But the police had closed off the road and wouldn't allow anyone through because a brush fire was aggressively spreading. Heidi got word that the men at the camp were safe, so she turned the car around and headed for home. The afternoon sky was filled with ash, and a wall of fire barreled over the ridge and across the fields like a freight train. The blaze was a raging inferno of eighty-mile-per-hour winds roaring like an angry, out-of-control locomotive. Heidi didn't have much time, but she ran to help her landlord evacuate dozens of horses and other animals on the ranch. In less than an hour, the fire had traveled four miles, burned thousands of acres, and was now within fifty yards of Heidi's front door. The weight of the smoke and ash was intense, making it difficult to see and breathe.

Heidi ran to her house to grab what she could. The first thing in the car was a suitcase that held the costumes of Gladys, Penelope, and Jan—characters she plays for Shadow Mountain Community Church's drama ministry, also regularly featured characters on *Turning Point* Television. She loaded in the costumes—feeling as if she were saving close friends from certain death. These were immediately followed by her cat and rabbit, some clothes, and a small collection of sentimental items. She drove away from her home—the flames within feet of her tires.

Heidi drove directly to her parents' house, but a few hours later they were evacuated from there as well. Her parents were now following her in a caravan stuck in the traffic jam trying to escape the flames that were enveloping the countryside. Heidi's gas light flicked on empty, and her parents' car was beginning to overheat. She prayed to God for a miracle. God provided—the police opened up the opposite lane and motioned for them to take it. They passed hundreds of cars and made it to safety and a gas station.

After leaving Ramona, the first place Heidi wanted to go was Shadow Mountain Community Church. It was late and no one was there, but it was comforting just to be sitting in the parking lot of the place she knew and loved. After some hours of searching, Heidi and her parents were able to find a hotel that would allow their pets. What they thought would be an overnight stay turned out to be an entire week. They were not allowed back to their homes while firefighters continued to battle the wildfires, which would ultimately force more than 1 million people to evacuate, burn over 500,000 acres, and destroy more than 1,600 homes.

Heidi's landlord called her a few days later to deliver devastating news—her house had been completely destroyed. As Heidi hung up the phone, tears streamed down her face because she, like many other people in her area, had been unable to obtain insurance for her home. Living in an area of open land, surrounded by brush, insurance companies categorized her home as "an enormous fire hazard." Heidi also found out that day that Oakbridge had been badly damaged.

After a week, residents were allowed back to their homes. With her home burned to the ground, Heidi went to live at her parents' house, a stay that would last six months. Due to fire damage at Oakbridge, she would not be able to return to work for two months.

Desolated by the loss of her house and all her possessions, Heidi never questioned God's purpose. She was immensely thankful that she and her family were safe and unharmed. There was no questioning that God is sovereign and in control of everything. She knew that bad things happen—even to followers of Christ. Being a Christian, serving in the church, and committing her life to sharing the truth of Christ with others did not exclude her from trials and hardship—and never would she want it to. Even in the midst of her loss, she knew that everything would be okay, and God would receive the glory for it all.

Heidi's response to the tragedy is, "I don't deserve His countless blessings in my life. He saved me from hell, so I could handle a little house fire."

Some things in life are hard to understand. People ask all the time, "Why does God let bad things happen to good people?" But Heidi understood that God cares for her, that He is faithful, and He promises to provide. Comforted by His love and assurance, she didn't ask God why everything happened, trusting in His will, but she did ask how—"How am I going to replace everything?" She knew to place her trust in the Lord, but little did she know or expect the resounding answer God had for that question.

Support in the form of cards, gifts, clothing, and money came pouring in as people heard about Heidi's situation. Her family was a great help and encouragement to her during that time. She received many contributions from the congregation at Shadow Mountain and the people at Turning Point. The burden of replacing the things she had lost was lifted. God provided her with all her needs—and then some—through the generosity of others. She never cried so many tears of joy as with the outpouring of love and support from the people around her.

Heidi recalls that "it's one thing to know the Lord will provide, and another thing entirely to experience it firsthand in an obvious and tangible way."

Through this experience, Heidi learned to appreciate the little things in life. The shoes in the giveaway pile that weren't stylish suddenly looked a lot more fashionable. The old dresser with tattered finish and stubborn drawers was now perfectly fine. And that small stain on her shirt was barely visible. It was hard losing almost everything, but Heidi realized that it was just stuff, and when she lost all her possessions, there was nowhere to go but up.

God gives and takes away, but He also gives again. He takes great delight in providing for us, His children. We cannot control the acts of nature that are capable of destroying the things we have. But we can take comfort in the fact that God is there to pour out His devotion and provision in the midst of our loss.

CHAPTER 9

The World in Chaos—
Fighting the Loss of Hope

*The eternal God is your refuge, and underneath
are the everlasting arms; He will thrust out the enemy
from before you, and will say, "Destroy!"*

DEUTERONOMY 33:27

THE SOVEREIGN

From the end of the earth I will cry to You, when
my heart is overwhelmed; lead me to the rock that is higher
than I. For You have been a shelter for me, a strong tower
from the enemy. I will abide in Your tabernacle forever;
I will trust in the shelter of Your wings.

PSALM 61:2-4

If you're old enough to have watched the dramatic newscasts as the Iron Curtain fell and the old Soviet Union broke apart, you probably remember the Polish labor leader, Lech Walesa, who became Poland's president and a Nobel Prize Laureate. Recently Walesa gave a speech in Chicago in which he declared the world has lost hope in America as a moral leader.

"The United States is only one superpower," he said. "Today they lead the world. Nobody has doubts about it, militarily. They also lead economically, but they're getting weak. They don't lead morally and politically anymore. The world has no leadership. The United States was always the last resort and hope for all other nations. There was the hope, whenever something was going wrong, one could count on the United States. Today we (have) lost that hope."[23]

People around the world are losing hope, not just in America but in the future. A recent article in the *London Telegraph* warned that the world is near the point of fiscal disintegration, and the newspaper

23   Kathleen Gilbert. "Lech Walesa: World has Lost Hope of America's Moral Leadership"at http://www.lifesite-news.com/ldn/2010/feb/10020506.html, accessed March 1, 2010.

used the home state of President Barack Obama as an example. "The state is in utter crisis," said one congressional delegate. "We are next to bankruptcy." Illinois has been paying bills with unfunded vouchers for months. A fifth of the buses have stopped. Libraries are closing one day a week.

> People around the world are losing hope, not just in America but in the future.

Schools are unable to pay teachers and preparing for massive layoffs, prompting one school administrator to say, "It's a catastrophe." Sheriff's patrol cars have been repossessed, law enforcement officers have been let go, and prisons are refusing to accept more inmates.

Other states are in even worse shape, but let's not just pick on America. Hungary, Ukraine, the Baltics, and the Balkans are in crisis. Greece's financial collapse earlier this year threatened to drag down all of Europe. Dubai's meltdown threatened to pull down the nations of the Middle East. "These are epic warning signs," said the newspaper, "with echoes of 1931."[24]

Is there any hope for us? No one is immune from global catastrophe, whether it's looming economic depression, natural disasters, or military and political turmoil. Even Nicolas Cage, one of Hollywood's most successful actors, suffered acute financial meltdown by overextending himself in a troubled economy. He bought castles, mansions, cars, and planes as if they were candies at a dime store; and Cage suddenly found himself with far more obligations than income. Banks, mortgage companies, creditors, and Uncle Sam all wanted his last dime. The actor told the press, "The first thing you think is 'This can't be true.' I want to crawl up and hide at the end of the world."

24   Ambrose Evans-Pritchard. "Don't Go Wobbly On Us Now, Ben Bernanke. February 28, 2010, at http://www.telegraph.co.uk/finance/comment/ambroseevans_pritchard/7338857/Dont-go-wobbly-on-us-now-Ben-Bernanke.html

The biblical character Job felt the same way. "Where then is my hope?" he said. "As for my hope, who can see it?" (Job 17:15)

But it's not just the economy. America's vice president recently confided that he worries constantly about a

Is there any hope for us? terrorist attack, but not necessarily another 9-11 type massive assault. Though such a high-profile act of terrorism is possible, it's the "lone bomber" scenario that keeps many officials awake at night—a suicide bomber on a bus, at a school, in a shopping mall, or sports arena.

And let's not forget those 23,574 known nuclear warheads in the world. It would take about five hundred of them to kill every human being on earth, but the detonation of just one of them would change our world forever.

We can add other headlines to the mix: modern slavery, sexual perversion and exploitation, child abuse, wars, international conflict, widespread natural disasters, radical Islam, militant atheism, and maybe global climate change (depending on your views about that).

SPILLED MILK (OR WATER)

But sometimes it's not global issues that send us into an orbit of despair; it's something as simple as a glass of spilled milk. Or water. A reader to the advice columnist of the *Washington Post* recently wrote about dropping a full glass of water on the living room carpet. Why that should provoke her husband, I'm not sure, but the couple had a knock-down, drag-out fight. Afterward they both wondered why they had so overreacted. That led to their wondering if they were fit to have kids, and somehow they just spiraled into despair. The writer ended her letter saying, "Is there any hope for us?

I feel really lost and would appreciate any counsel and perspective you could offer."[25]

THE IRRESISTIBLE UPDRAFT OF BIBLICAL HOPE

Millions of people today are wondering if there is any hope, and the problems are a great deal worse than spilled water. But before you quit reading out of utter despair, I'm going to shift gears. Despite its title, this chapter isn't really about the loss of hope. It's about how to live in a chaotic world without losing hope. There are lots of reasons to be discouraged, but there are better reasons to be hopeful.

Every generation since Adam has faced calamity. Within its epochs, the Bible records a long history of wars, plagues, famines, corruption, depravity, suffering, war, and wrongdoing. Yet God is in control. He reigns and rules and overrules. He has a plan, and His Bible is a book of hope. Our Lord is a God of hope; and when we walk with Him, we find ourselves lifted by the irresistible updraft of biblical hope.

The writer of Psalm 42 tapped into this when he wrote, "Why are you cast down, O my soul? And why are you disquieted within me? Hope in God, for I shall yet praise Him for the help of His countenance."

Dr. Martyn Lloyd-Jones, in commenting on this Psalm, said, "The first thing we have to learn is what the psalmist learned—we must take ourselves in hand. This man was not content just to lie down and commiserate with himself. He does something about it, he takes himself in hand. . . . He talks to himself. . . . I say that we must talk to ourselves instead of allowing

> Every generation since Adam has faced calamity.

25   Carolyn Hex Style Columnist, February 22, 2010, *The Washington Post* at http://www.washingtonpost.com/wp-dyn/content/article/2010/02/21/AR2010022102983.html, accessed March 1, 2010.

'ourselves' to talk to us. . . . Have you realized that most of your unhappiness in life is due to the fact that you are listening to yourself instead of talking to yourself?"[26]

The good doctor is right. We have to learn to preach to ourselves. We have to learn to encourage ourselves in the Lord. We must learn to search out and claim God's promises for our present needs and future fears. We must ask the Holy Spirit to make those verses so real in our minds they'll lift our spirits like giant balloons of spiritual helium.

The psalmist said, "I will hope continually, and will praise You yet more and more" (Psalm 71:14).

Proverbs 10:28 says: "The hope of the righteous will be gladness."

Jeremiah said, "Blessed is the man who trusts in the Lord, and whose hope is the Lord. For he shall be like a tree planted by the waters, which spreads out its roots by the river" (Jeremiah 17:7-8).

Lamentation 3:21-26 says, "This I recall to my mind, therefore I have hope . . . His compassions fail not. They are new every morning; great is Your faithfulness. 'The Lord is my portion,' says my soul, "therefore I hope in Him. . . .' It is good that one should hope and wait quietly."

Romans 5:5 says, "Hope does not disappoint."

The apostle Paul wrote, "Now may the God of hope fill you with all joy and peace in believing, that you may abound in hope by the power of the Holy Spirit" (Romans 15:13).

The Bible is filled with hopeful verses, and each one is special because God knows we sometimes feel hopeless. According to the American Psychological Association, work and money are the biggest stress factors for three of four adults. Research shows that people are quicker to overeat, drink, gamble, and smoke during times of

---

26   D. Martyn Lloyd-Jones, *Spiritual Depression* (Grand Rapids: Eerdmans, 1965), 20.

financial stress. They visit doctors more. They have trouble sleeping and complain more of stress-induced stomach pain and headaches. The *Washington Post* reported that suicide rates are on the rise again after more than a decade of dropping. The suspected culprit? Money trouble. "What I hear from my clients and colleagues suggests that the financial downturn and continued uncertainty have overtaxed us emotionally," said Michael Oberschneider, a psychologist writing in the *Washington Post*.[27]

But there's no prescription any better than God's verses of hope. Hebrews 6:19 says, "This hope we have as an anchor of the soul, both sure and steadfast."

Peter said that we have been born again into a "living hope" (1 Peter 1:3). Romans 12:12 tells us to be "rejoicing in hope."

The hope-message of the Bible is so stalwart and strong that it even uplifts us on the deathbed. A Brooklyn pastor of an earlier era, Ichabod Spencer, told of being called to the bedside of a woman who was dying. He found her bedroom filled with family and friends who had gathered to see her die. Making his way through the crowd, he stood by her bed and could see she was in the last agonies of death. She was bolstered up on her pillow, gasping for breath, almost suffocated by asthma, and the whole bed shook as she convulsed with palpitations of the heart. Reverend Spencer called her name and said, "You seem to be very sick."

> The hope-message of the Bible is stalwart and strong.

"Yes," she said, "I am dying."

"And are you ready to die?" he asked.

---

27   Michael Oberschneider, "Loss of Wealth Can Disrupt Mental Health," in the Washington Post, April 28, 2009, at http://www.washingtonpost.com/wp-dyn/content/article/2009/04/27/AR2009042702892.html.

"She lifted her eyes to him and said very earnestly and triumphantly between gasps for breath, "God knows . . . I have taken Him at His Word . . . and . . . I am not afraid to die."

Every phrase was difficult, but the glow on her face was wondrous. Reverend Spencer quoted Scriptures to her and prayed for several minutes; and then he turned to leave, but she reached out and caught his hand. Gasping for breath, she said, "I wanted to tell you . . . that I can . . . trust . . . in God . . . while I am dying. You have often told me . . . He would not forsake me. . . . And now I find it is true. I am at peace. I die willingly and happily."

Reverend Spencer left the room.

But the woman did not die. To everyone's surprise, she recovered and lived for many years. But no one ever forgot her "dying" testimony. Her hope gave her buoyancy for both dying and living.[28]

According to Isaiah 40, those who hope in the Lord shall renew their strength and mount up with wings like eagles. In a world in which we're beset by burdens big and small, we have the strong gusts of hope, catching our wings and sending us soaring heavenward as God's hopeful, joyful people.

So let's sanctify the Lord God in our hearts and always be ready to give an answer to everyone in this despairing world who asks us a reason for the hope that is within us.

Hope thou in God!

28   Ichabod Spencer, *A Pastor's Sketches* (Vestavia Hills, AL: Solid Ground Christian Books, 2001), 58.

THE SUFFERING

Personal Story—Jeremy Wood

There is a well-worn phrase that simply states, "War is hell." The quote is traditionally credited to Union Army General William Tecumseh Sherman who wrote it in a letter during the Civil War. But if, as a photojournalist for the Navy, you had seen more than your fair share of the current chaos and hopelessness caused by warfare in the world today, you'd agree the statement is still relevant. Yes, warfare exemplifies the corruption of man, but it cannot eliminate the sovereignty of God—even in the bleakest of situations. Meet Jeremy Wood.

Jeremy was sent on a combat tour in 2003 to Sadr City outside of Baghdad, Iraq. He didn't know any specifics, only that Sadr was one of the worst assignments in the war-torn country. The journey to the city was treacherous. Their convoy of military vehicles drove between buildings from which insurgents regularly threw grenades down into their vehicles, past alleys where enemies waited to fire rocket-propelled grenades, and around road blocks made of burning oil, feces, or anything their foes could use to slow them down. A sickening smell filled the sandy, abrasive air as a trail of rancid black liquid flowed down the streets.

Upon reaching his destination, Forward Operating Base Eagle outside Sadr, Jeremy assisted in awarding Purple Hearts to twelve wounded soldiers. What a way to be welcomed to Iraq! It was a palpable reminder that he was in the thick of the war effort. FOB Eagle was the most decorated camp at the time, and it didn't take long for

Jeremy to discover why there were so many medals being awarded at this base. He found that sleep was intermittent at best as insurgents launched twenty to thirty mortar shells into the camp each night. The soldiers were ordered to wear body armor at all times—not to save them from being killed, but to keep their body intact if they were hit. Lying in his bunk with full armor each night, Jeremy watched a crack in the ceiling spread a little more with each deafening rumble of incoming enemy artillery. He couldn't help but think that the building could buckle in an instant, the fractured ceiling collapsing without warning. When would his time be? In the moments he found himself outside the protection of the structure, Jeremy found shelter under any rock he could find and became accustomed to sleeping on and under concrete—sometimes crawling in concrete niches to catch a quick nap.

Many soldiers were wounded and killed in Sadr City. Those who survived bear the emotional and mental scars just from being there. Jeremy served in many war-torn areas, but none were as frightening as Sadr. Months later in Fallujah, Jeremy was assigned to mortuary affairs, a branch that is responsible for collecting, counting, and burying the bodies of their enemies killed in combat. On the first day of his new assignment, the death toll reached more than four hundred. The soldiers buried their foes in traditional Muslim fashion in the city cemetery until the sound of bullets hissing past them stopped their efforts. As they returned fire on the insurgents, Jeremy found himself filled with disgust. He never imagined he would be caught in the midst of gunfire on the sacred ground of a cemetery. Were there no rules? Had morality and virtue been thrown out the window?

These troubling thoughts nearly consumed Jeremy as he and the other men fought for their lives—seeing things that no one should ever have to see. The depravity of mankind was on display before them. Yet, even in these darkest hours, even in the midst of unspeakable monstrosities, Jeremy could clearly see the Lord at work.

Out on a patrol one day, Jeremy's convoy was stopped along a highway. He looked out his window and saw an improvised explosive device (IED) right outside his door. (IEDs are homemade roadside bombs, often planted along the ground, that have killed a large number of soldiers in Iraq.) He realized that they had to get moving; the IED could explode any second. Just as they pulled out of range, the IED exploded—decimating both lanes of the road to rubble. The place where Jeremy had been sitting was now a crater—God was at work.

Although none of Jeremy's assignments would ever be considered safe, some were worse than others. One station in particular was the sight of regular insurgent attacks on U.S. patrols. In just a short time, Jeremy had been spared during seven different barrages. As a result, one day his commanding officers decided to take his truck off of a scheduled patrol. With the unexpected free time, Jeremy went to chapel. That is where he heard the call from the base's loud speakers—the convoy sent in his place had been ambushed, leaving seven of his comrades dead and six wounded. Jeremy can't explain by his own reasoning why that IED failed to go off outside his door or why he was taken off the besieged patrol at the last minute. He can't empirically rationalize how, out of the countless bullets shot at him, he was never hit. The only explanation is a supernatural one. God's hand was active on that battlefield, even in the midst of war, even when all around him destruction and death were prevailing. Some may explain it as luck, but Jeremy knows it was not just good fortune. It was God's intervention, His miraculous intercession on the front line. There is no place that God won't go; in fact, it seems that the places where we think God should never be are the very places in which He is seen most clearly.

But God's protective cover over Jeremy opens up a new line of questions. Why was Jeremy spared when a Christian soldier next to him was shot? How could God choose to intervene to save one person, but let another die nearby? Why would God even put Jeremy there in the first place? Those are hard questions to answer. In trying to ponder questions such as these, we must remember, we aren't God and we cannot begin to understand His plan. Jeremy really doesn't require an answer to the questions many would ask; he already knows why—because God is sovereign. No further explanation is needed. God put him in bombed-out Sadr and the chaos of Fallujah for a purpose. Is Jeremy bitter with God, that He would be so unloving to send him to such a place? No. In fact, Jeremy thanks the Lord for His provision during those difficult times. The hardships in this life will lead him, and those around him, to a better end.

Who would ever choose adversity? None of us! But Jeremy understands that he was specifically used by God for a distinct purpose. He has had the opportunity to interact with many people in the military, sharing his faith through his words and his life. And he has learned so much from fellow Christians who have been an example and encouragement to him. War has strengthened his will and taught him that he cannot do everything on his own. Asking for help was always difficult; but now Jeremy asks without hesitation, especially from the One who can help the most—the Lord. This doesn't mean that Jeremy is free from difficulty, as he still suffers from elements of post-traumatic stress disorder, but he is improving each day. He still carries memories of fallen friends and traumatic images and sounds that are exhausting to recall, but he is not alone—he turns them over to the Lord.

Without God's active assistance, Jeremy knows he would fail. He could not handle the tragedies of the world without the knowledge of eternity. He thanks God for what he has and what he one day will inherit in heaven. He is grateful to have every functioning part of his body—something that some of his friends do not have. For now he lives with memories he would like to forget, but those memories are also a reminder of the loving care of his Savior who brought him safely through every battle.

War may be hell, but there is another aphorism that says "There are no atheists in a foxhole." Jeremy's faith gives him something to fight for and Someone to turn to. Watching fellow soldiers on the battle-field who struggled to survive combat without a hope or belief in God was difficult to observe. Jeremy acknowledges that it was his faith and God's provision that delivered him through those difficult times. It is the Lord who has provided Jeremy strength and solace. The world is filled with war, hatred, and strife, but God is with us in the most despairing moments of our lives to demonstrate His unending love and glory. The world may be in chaos, but in God we can have peace in our hearts.

CHAPTER 10

Why, God?—Struggling With the Loss of Faith

Behold, I am the LORD, the God of all flesh.

Is there anything too hard for Me?

JEREMIAH 32:27

THE SOVEREIGN

Jesus said to him, "If you can believe, all things
are possible to him who believes."

MARK 9:23

When the body of American president John F. Kennedy arrived
in Washington from Dallas on November 22, 1963, an autopsy was
performed, and then the casket was brought to the White House. Mrs.
Kennedy asked the attendants to open the casket, and when Bobby
Kennedy, the Attorney General of the United States, looked down into
the lifeless face of his brother, he collapsed. That night in the White
House, an aide heard Bobby sobbing, "Why, God, why?"[29]

From the halls of the White House to the humblest hovel in the
poorest country, all of humanity is interlocked by the question: Why?
That three-letter word expresses
our deepest questions in a simple
one-syllable term. It's one of the first
words we learn—just ask any parent
whose child is in the "Why?" phase.
It's the word our teenagers use when
they begin questioning our authority
and demanding justification for our rules. It's one of the questions we
ask during life's final stages in the hospice or sick room. It's a query of
philosophers, the mystery of theologians, and the perplexity of the ages.

> From the halls of the
> White House to the
> humblest hovel all of
> humanity is interlocked
> by the question: Why?

---

29 Ralph G. Martin, *A Hero for Our Time* (New York: Macmillan, 1983) n.p.

It's a biblical question. As we read through the stories of the heroes of Scripture, we often find this word on their lips.

- *Moses prayed, "Lord, why have You brought trouble on this people? Why is it You have sent me?"* (Exodus 5:22).
- *Joshua cried, "Alas, Lord God, why have You brought this people over the Jordan at all—to deliver us into the hand of the Amorites, to destroy us?"* (Joshua 7:7).
- *Gideon cried, "Why then has all this happened to us?"* (Judges 6:13).
- *Job cried, "Why did I not die at birth?"* (Job 3:11).
- *The psalmist wrote, "Why do You stand afar off, O Lord? Why do You hide in times of trouble?"* (Psalm 10:1).
- *David prayed, "Why are You so far from helping Me, and from the words of my groaning?"* (Psalm 22:1).
- *Asaph asked, "O God, why have You cast us off forever?"* (Psalm 74:1).
- *Nehemiah asked, "Why is the house of God forsaken?"* (Nehemiah 13:11).
- *Isaiah asked, "O Lord, why have You made us stray from Your ways?"* (Isaiah 63:17).
- *Jeremiah mourned, "Why have You stricken us so that there is no healing for us?"* (Jeremiah 14:19).
- *And Jesus cried out on the cross, saying, "My God, My God, why have You forsaken Me?"* (Matthew 27:46).

Anne Graham Lotz put it well in her little book *Why*, when she wrote, "Why does God let bad things happen to good people? To innocent people? To helpless people? To defenseless people?

To children? To me? Sometimes His ways seem so hard to understand!"[30]

If we don't figure out how to process the *whys* of life, we'll end up cynical, resulting in a catastrophic loss of faith. If we don't answer correctly, we'll grow bitter, resulting in a darkened personality. If we don't trust God with our *whys*, we'll grow pessimistic like Edgar Allen Poe in his epic poem, "The Raven":

> *Is there—is there balm in Gilead?*
> *—tell me—tell me, I implore!*
> *Quoth the raven, "Nevermore." . . .*
> *And my soul from out that shadow*
> *that lies floating on the floor*
> *Shall be lifted—nevermore!*

WE'LL TRUST TODAY

The Christian's word is: Evermore. We believe in hope, in God's ultimate Lordship over heaven and earth. We believe He understands all that confounds us, and that His knowledge has no limits. In Christ are hidden all the mysteries of wisdom and knowledge. We believe He has the capacity of working all things for the good to those who love Him. We know He works all things according to the ultimate purposes of His counsel. We consider "all is right that seems most wrong if it be His sweet will." Not a sparrow falls to the ground without His seeing it. Not a problem arises without His knowing it.

---

30   Anne Graham Lotz, *Why?* (Nashville: Thomas Nelson, 2004), 3.

Never a trial that He is not there,
Never a burden that He doth not bear,
Never a sorrow that He doth not share,
Moment by moment, I'm under His care.[31]

The psalmist said, "When my father and my mother forsake me, then the Lord will take care of me" (Psalm 27:10). The Bible tells us to cast all our cares on Him, for He cares for us (1 Peter 5:7). Our insights are faulty, our perspective limited, our minds small. There is a broader reality that God, in His omniscience, understands perfectly; and that's why Proverbs 3:5 tells us to trust in the Lord with all our hearts and to lean not on our own understanding.

It's often been said that when we can't trace God's hand, we can trust His heart. Faith is the substance of things hoped for and the evidence of things not seen (Hebrews 11:1). It is being fully convinced that what God has promised, He is able also to perform (Romans 4:21). It is believing that there will be a fulfillment of those things that are told us from the Lord (Luke 1:45).

When we can't trace God's hand, we can trust His heart.

All our *whys* were swallowed up in the one Jesus uttered at Calvary. Whatever our problem, we can look to the cross; whatever our burden, we strengthen our faith by doing as John did, stooping and gazing into the empty tomb.

In 1939, William Sangster assumed leadership of Westminster Central Hall, a Methodist church near London's Westminster Abbey.

---

31   Daniel W. Whittle, "Moment by Moment," in LifeWay Worship Project: Baptist Hymnal (Nashville: LifeWay, n.d.), 159.

During his first worship service, he announced to his stunned congregation that Britain and Germany were officially at war. He quickly converted the church basement into an air raid shelter; and for 1,688 nights, Sangster ministered to the various needs of all kinds of people. At the same time, he somehow managed to write, to preach gripping sermons, to earn a Ph.D., and to lead hundreds to Christ. He became known as Wesley's successor in London and was esteemed as the most beloved British preacher of his era.

Sometime after the war, Sangster was diagnosed with progressive muscular atrophy. For three years he slowly died, becoming progressively more paralyzed, finally able to move only two fingers. But his attitude didn't falter, for when first learning of his illness, Sangster made four rules for himself: "I will never complain. I will keep the home bright. I will count my blessings. I will try to turn it to gain."

He did all those things based on the constant presence of Christ with him. And thus the work of God was displayed in his life, and in his death. Even when we don't understand, we can trust. And when we trust, joy breaks through the clouds like rays of sunshine.

WE'LL UNDERSTAND LATER

We can also reassure ourselves that someday we'll understand it all better. There's a great lesson about this in the biblical Book of Job. Next time you pick up your Bible and turn to the Book of Job (especially if you look at a newer translation), notice the first two chapters are narrative. They are history, written in the style of prose. Then starting with chapter 3, the literary form changes to poetry, and the dialogues between Job, his friends, and the Lord are given in versified, poetic language. This runs from chapter 3 to the first part of chapter 42. At the very end of the book, in chapter 42, the text changes back to narrative and the book concludes.

This is the only book of the Bible structured like this, but this shift from narrative to poetry to narrative gives us a clue to Job's faith. In the opening narrative, God explains to us the *reason* Job was being attacked. Satan was accusing him before God in the realms of heaven, a fact Job himself did not know at the time. In the last chapter, we're told the *outcome* of Job's sorrows and the blessings that crowned the last half of his years, which Job only experienced after his suffering.

So the narratives in chapters 1 and 2 tell us the *reason* for Job's sorrows, and the conclusion in chapter 42 tells us the *results*. But Job didn't have access to that information during his trials. So from chapters 3 to 41, he and his friends tried to work through his emotions without knowing the reasons for them or the results of them—information that only God possessed at that time. These chapters are given poetically to show us the depth of the feelings behind the words. As we read through this book, we find 290 questions. Every chapter of Job except chapter 29 contains at least one question mark. The word "Why?" occurs 29 times in the book. But even though Job had far more questions than answers, he kept affirming and reaffirming his faith.

He said, "The Lord gave, and the Lord has taken away; blessed be the name of the Lord" (Job 1:21).

He said, "Shall we indeed accept good from God, and shall we not accept adversity?" (Job 2:10)

He said, "Though He slay me, yet will I trust Him" (Job 13:15).

He said, "I know that my Redeemer lives, and He shall stand at last on the earth; and after my skin is destroyed, this I know, that in my flesh I shall see God" (Job 19:25-26).

He said, "He knows the way that I take; when He has tested me, I shall come forth as gold" (Job 23:10).

Faith works best in adverse times; indeed, without adversity there's little need for faith. If our faith doesn't work in the darkness, it's not much good in the light. And so we trust Him today, knowing that someday we'll understand it all—if not now, then; if not here, there.

Many years ago, a man named Maxwell Cornelius, a building contractor in Pittsburg, had an accident and his leg was amputated. As time went by, he became a minister of the Gospel, but he went through many other hardships. Out of his difficulties he wrote the poem with which I want to end this chapter. Perhaps it's a stanza that will comfort and strengthen you today:

> *Not now, but in the coming years,*
> *It may be in the better land,*
> *We'll read the meaning of our tears,*
> *And there, some time, we'll understand.*

THE SUFFERING

Personal Story—Bob "Sully" Sullivan

*O*ur relationship with the Lord is a complex and elaborate journey, filled with its own series of highs and lows. Why some choose to journey away from God for a season is hard to understand. This is the journey of one man who has walked in the valley of destruction, but has been restored by the mercy and grace of our loving God. Meet Bob Sullivan.

Bob Sullivan, known as "Sully" to his friends and the audience of his radio show, is a successful radio personality who hosts a nationally syndicated financial advice talk show broadcasting from San Diego, California. From the outside he looks like a guy who has it all—a career he loves, a loving wife, and two beautiful daughters. But only a few years ago, people would have said just the opposite—he was in a fight for everything he wanted for his life, battling addiction and trying to hold his life together on all fronts.

A native of San Diego, Sully came to know the Lord through the outreach of his next door neighbors, Harold and Ann Throckmorton, who took him to church every Sunday when he was a child. He became a Christian and was baptized in 1972 at the age of twelve. In middle school and high school, Sully took part in a number of Christian youth programs. A talented musician even as a child, he played guitar for many of the events. As a teenager, Sully was the Boy Wonder—a staple of his Christian youth programs, class president, the lead in all the plays at school, and the captain of the football team. When it came time for college, he attended a private Catholic university in San Diego that offered him a music scholarship. Once there, he took theology classes, which left his nineteen-year-old mind struggling to reconcile the conflicting doctrines of various Christian denominations. Theological concepts and questions buzzed in his head, destabilizing his faith and the knowledge of God with which he had grown up. He started attending a church with his college friends who were passionate about the Lord on Sundays, but who regularly became drunk (wasted/high) at parties during the week. Struggling to rationalize how believers could live such a dichotomous faith, he was perplexed. If God was so powerful, and He could transform the lives of His followers, why were his friends acting as if they didn't know God at all? Sully surmised that Christianity was an empty belief and walked away from God—a dangerous journey that would last twenty years.

After college, Sully pursued a career in radio broadcasting. Without the Lord as an active part of his life, he walked a destructive path. He started partying regularly, getting heavily involved in drugs and alcohol. He became addicted to Ritalin (a prescription drug similar to the street drug "speed" given to people who suffer from Attention Deficit Disorder) and other illicit drugs. As a result, he showed up to most of his morning radio shifts hung over. His family life fell apart, and he set a horrible example for his daughters, who were both in elementary school at the time. He was living a lie. Known on his radio show as the "Money Guy" who gave financial advice, he was losing his job and was close to bankruptcy. His actions were destroying everything he wanted for his life.

During that time, every Tuesday night about thirty cars crowded into the cul-de-sac in his neighborhood—a weekly cause of frustration for Sully. Someone must be having weekly parties, he thought, loathing his neighbor who was hosting whatever was going on over there. In reality, the visitors taking all the parking in Sully's neighborhood weren't having parties—they were Christians having a weekly Bible study. Also unknown to him was that he was the object of their prayers, well known in the community as the crazy radio guy who partied too hard. None of them would have guessed that Bob Sullivan had grown up a passionate Christian—he certainly wasn't living that way now.

Sully's life turned around on Easter Sunday of 2003. That Sunday his wife insisted that he attend church with the family—he complied, albeit hung over and spiritually kicking and screaming. Many people in the congregation were familiar with his reputation and he knew it, a fact that added to his discomfort. As the pastor preached, Sully felt like he was the only one in the room. He did not want to be sitting there, knowing he had chosen the destructive path he was living away from God, but at the same time it felt like home. It was almost like God was tapping him on the shoulder telling to come back to Him. It was a catharsis, the purging of all the resistance he had built up over the past twenty years. Knowing he needed to get his life in order, Sully was ready to fall back into his Father's care and guidance. Picking up the faith he had left lying in the gutter for two decades, he called the pastor the next day. He advised Sully to get into a recovery group, regardless of whether or not he thought he was an alcoholic or a drug addict. So Sully joined a recovery group at his church, meeting with other men struggling with similar issues. As he met more people at church, his life began intersecting with the lives of the members of that small group on his street that had irritated him so much. Those believers who had been praying for him belonged to his new church! The power that seemed so absent from the body of believers when he was in college was suddenly concretely evident through the power of prayer and the acting forgiveness of God.

Sully became friends with fellow believers at church. One of those friends, Greg, regularly met with him to play guitar. At one of their music sessions, Greg brought a man with him who, unknown to Sully, was the leader of the church worship team. The guest was impressed with Sully's talent and suggested he join the praise band. The thought made Sully cringe. He wanted nothing to do with that and vowed he would never play music for a church. He knew deep down that being a part of the worship ministry would require him to be accountable and to walk the walk as an example to others. The challenge of openly representing himself, his faith, the Lord, and his church was over-whelming. But God worked on his heart, and Sully agreed to sing a solo at the church's Christmas service. The following month he was a part of the worship team. After about a year and a half with the band, they recorded a CD which garnered attention and favorable reviews around San Diego. Originally so averse to the idea, Sully has now been the worship leader for three years. God put Bob Sullivan on the fast track of faith, bringing him out of his brokenness and into a meaningful relationship with Him.

Sully is grateful that he got a second chance, something a lot of people don't get. It is by God's mercy that he is alive today. Accountability has been an integral part of Sully's faith, with many friends and mentors leading and helping him from a crawl of belief to a walk of faith. Without the constant accountability, he would not have been able to overcome his addictions. He experienced the loss of his old self, but was given a new and blessed life by the Lord. He had chosen a destructive path, but God in His mercy provided grace and restored Sully. God had a plan for him and continues to have a plan for him. The Lord is working in Sully as he attempts to serve Him and to be His hands and feet. He is encouraged by a Francis of Assisi quote "Preach the Gospel at all times and use words, if necessary." Sully is finding that this comes easier as he matures in his Christian walk.

Bob "Sully" Sullivan has traveled a difficult journey, but has found that the Savior is always there with open arms to accept those who come to Him, even those like Bob, who abandoned their relationship with God. The Lord is enthusiastic to forgive and receive His children back into His loving arms.

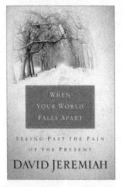

When Your World Falls Apart

Drawing from the deep truths of the Psalms, David Jeremiah identifies the traumatic events that inspired this writing and finds his focus changing. Instead of asking "Why?" he began to ask "What, O Lord? What do you have to teach me? What would you have me do?" If you're walking through difficult times, this book may serve as a helpful resource.

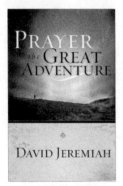

Prayer—The Great Adventure

This study on prayer explores the pattern of prayer Jesus gave to His disciples and examines how we can follow that pattern and put it into practice in our lives. As you study this prayer and begin to implement the teaching of our Lord in your own life, you'll become more thankful for what He has done, and you will begin to see His power at work. This study will reveal what a remarkable God we have!

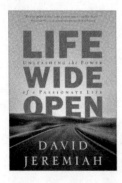

Life Wide Open

Modern culture teaches us to compartmentalize our lives. But God created us to be holistic beings who, when filled with His life and power, exude passion and enthusiasm about everything we do. In *Life Wide Open*, Dr. David Jeremiah discusses eleven different areas from faith to work to life to humility to help you live the abundant life Christ came to give.

God, I Need Some Answers—Life Lessons from Psalms

The Psalms were written by people who struggled with many of the same things we face today, including guilt, anxiety, loneliness, fear, and frustration. In *God, I Need Some Answers—Life Lessons from Psalms,* Dr. David Jeremiah reveals God's answers to several of life's foundational questions, such as: Who Am I? or How Can I Be Happy? Each is answered from the richness of God's Word with life-changing applications for today in this special study from the Psalms.

Captured by Grace

Captured by Grace is all about the multifaceted jewel of grace. It will open up vistas of grace you may be unfamiliar with. Most Christians know they were saved by grace, but are not aware that they live by grace. Nor do they know that grace is the pathway leading them to their heavenly home for eternity. Grace is the past, present, and future of the Christian experience. If your Christian life is not what you know it could and should be, it may be lacking grace.